BECAUSE OF
Bethlehem

IN THE
MANGER

ALSO BY MAX LUCADO

BECAUSE OF
Bethlehem
LOVE IS BORN, HOPE IS HERE

IN THE
MANGER

25 INSPIRATIONAL
SELECTIONS *for* ADVENT

MAX LUCADO

THOMAS NELSON
Since 1798

Published in Nashville, Tennessee, by Thomas Nelson. Thomas Nelson is a registered trademark of HarperCollins Christian Publishing, Inc.

Thomas Nelson titles may be purchased in bulk for educational, business, fund-raising, or sales promotional use. For information, please e-mail SpecialMarkets@ThomasNelson.com.

For *Because of Bethlehem*, unless otherwise noted, Scripture quotations are taken from the Holy Bible, New International Version®, NIV®. Copyright © 1973, 1978, 1984, 2011 by Biblica, Inc.® Used by permission of Zondervan. All rights reserved worldwide. www.zondervan.com. The "NIV" and "New International Version" are trademarks registered in the United States Patent and Trademark Office by Biblica, Inc.®

For *In the Manger*, unless otherwise noted, Scripture quotations are taken from the New King James Version®. © 1982 by Thomas Nelson. Used by permission. All rights reserved.

Scripture quotations marked GNT are from the Good News Translation in Today's English Version—Second Edition. Copyright 1992 by American Bible Society. Used by permission. Scripture quotations marked THE MESSAGE are from *The Message*. Copyright © by Eugene H. Peterson 1993, 1994, 1995, 1996, 2000, 2001, 2002. Used by permission of Tyndale House Publishers, Inc. Scripture quotations marked NASB are from New American Standard Bible®. Copyright © 1960, 1962, 1963, 1968, 1971, 1972, 1973, 1975, 1977, 1995 by The Lockman Foundation. Used by permission. (www.Lockman.org). Scripture quotations marked NCV are from the New Century Version®. © 2005 by Thomas Nelson. Used by permission. All rights reserved. Scripture quotations marked NET are from the NET Bible®. Copyright © 1996–2006 by Biblical Studies Press, L.L.C. http://netbible.com. All rights reserved. Scripture quotations marked NIrV are from the Holy Bible, New International Reader's Version®, NIrV®. Copyright ©1995, 1996, 1998, 2014 by Biblica, Inc.® Used by permission of Zondervan. All rights reserved worldwide. www.zondervan.com. The "NIrV" and "New International Reader's Version" are trademarks registered in the United States Patent and Trademark Office by Biblica, Inc.® Scripture quotations marked NLT are from the *Holy Bible*, New Living Translation. © 1996, 2004, 2007, 2013 by Tyndale House Foundation. Used by permission of Tyndale House Publishers, Inc., Carol Stream, Illinois 60188. All rights reserved. Scripture quotations marked NRSV are from New Revised Standard Version Bible. Copyright © 1989 National Council of the Churches of Christ in the United States of America. Used by permission. All rights reserved. Scripture quotations marked RSV are from Revised Standard Version of the Bible. Copyright 1946, 1952, and 1971 National Council of the Churches of Christ in the United States of America. Used by permission. All rights reserved. Scripture quotations marked TLB are from The Living Bible. Copyright © 1971. Used by permission of Tyndale House Publishers, Inc., Carol Stream, Illinois 60188. All rights reserved. Scripture quotations marked THE VOICE are from The Voice™. © 2012 by Ecclesia Bible Society. Used by permission. All rights reserved. Note: Italics in quotations from The Voice are used to "indicate words not directly tied to the dynamic translation of the original language" but that "bring out the nuance of the original, assist in completing ideas, and . . . provide readers with information that would have been obvious to the original audience" (The Voice, preface). Scripture quotations marked WEB are from the World English Bible™. Public domain.

All hymns are taken from the public domain unless otherwise noted.

ISBN 978-1-4041-0599-7 (custom)

Printed in the United States of America

17 18 19 20 LSC 6 5 4 3 2 1

Contents

BECAUSE OF

Bethlehem

*Denalyn and I are honored to dedicate this book
to Randy and Rozanne Frazee.
Able workers.
Devoted servants.
Wonderful friends.*

Acknowledgments

Wise men, shepherds, and angels. They came to Joseph and Mary. They came to me as well. Thanks to the following folks, this book was completed.

Editors Liz Heaney and Karen Hill—Such diligence and patience.

Copy editor Carol Bartley—No error slips past your skillful eyes.

The management team of Steve and Cheryl Green—Truer friends cannot be found.

The TN publishing group led by Mark Schoenwald, David Moberg, LeeEric Fesko, and Liz Johnson—I sincerely appreciate your untiring support.

Consultants and publicists Greg and Susan Ligon and Jana Muntsinger—Every author should have your creative assistance.

Prayer warrior David Treat—Ever present, ever interceding. Just like Jesus.

The Oak Hills Church—Each time I step into the pulpit, I think, *Are they not tired of me yet?* But you keep showing up.

Administrative assistants Janie Padilla and Margaret Mechinus—Hour by hour solving problems, offering support. So valuable.

My family: Brett, Jenna, Andrea, Jeff, and Sara—You make this papa's heart burst with pride.

Grandbaby Rose—Your mom delivered you into the world at the time I delivered this book to be published. Your arrival is the one that matters! Welcome!

And dear, dear Denalyn—Because of you I've enjoyed Christmas every day for thirty-four years. Love you.

1

I Love Christmas

I love Christmas. Let the sleigh bells ring. Let the carolers sing. The more Santas the merrier. The more trees the better.

I love Christmas. The ho ho ho, the rooty toot toot, the thumpety, thump, thump, and the pa rum pa pum pum. The "Silent Night" and the sugarplums.

I don't complain about the crowded shops. I don't grumble at the jam-packed grocery store. The flight is full? The restaurant is packed? Well, it's Christmas.

And I love Christmas.

Bring on Scrooge, Cousin Eddie, and the "official Red Ryder, carbine-action, two-hundred shot range model air rifle." "You'll shoot your eye out!"

The tinsel and the clatter and waking up "to see what was the matter." Bing and his tunes. Macy's balloons. Mistletoe kisses, Santa Claus wishes, and favorite dishes. Holiday snows, warm winter clothes, and Rudolph's red nose.

I love Christmas.

I love it because somewhere someone will ask the

Christmas questions: What's the big deal about the baby in the manger? Who was he? What does his birth have to do with me? The questioner may be a child looking at a front-yard crèche. He may be a soldier stationed far from home. She may be a young mom who, for the first time, holds a child on Christmas Eve. The Christmas season prompts questions.

———⊗≫○———

> I love Christmas because somewhere someone will ask the Christmas questions: What's the big deal about the baby in the manger?

———⊗≫○———

I can remember the first time I asked those questions. I grew up in a small West Texas town, the son of a mechanic and a nurse. Never poor but certainly not affluent. My dad laid pipeline in the oil fields. Mom worked the three-to-eleven shift at the hospital. I followed my brother to elementary school every morning and played neighborhood ball in the afternoons.

Dad was in charge of dinner. My brother washed the dishes, and I was in charge of sweeping the floor. We boys took our baths by eight and were in bed by nine with permission to do one thing before turning out the lights. We could read.

The chest at the foot of our bed contained children's books. Big books, each with a glossy finish and bright pictures. The three bears lived in the chest. So did the big, bad wolf and seven dwarfs and a monkey with a lunch pail, whose name I don't recall. Somewhere in the chest, beneath the fairy tales, was a book about baby Jesus.

On the cover was a yellow-hayed manger. A star glowed above the stable. Joseph and a donkey, equally big eyed, stood nearby. Mary held a baby in her arms. She looked down at him, and he looked up at her, and I remember looking at them both.

My dad, a man of few words, had told my brother and me, "Boys, Christmas is about Christ."

In one of those bedtime, book-time moments, somewhere between the fairy tales and the monkey with the lunch pail, I thought about what he had said. I began asking the Christmas questions. In one way or another, I've been asking them ever since.

I love the answers I have found.

Like this one: God knows what it is like to be a human. When I talk to him about deadlines or long lines or tough times, he understands. He's been there. He's been *here*. Because of Bethlehem, I have a friend in heaven.

Because of Bethlehem, I have a Savior in heaven. Christmas begins what Easter celebrates. The child in the cradle became the King on the cross. And because he did, there are no marks on my record. Just grace. His offer has no fine print.

He didn't tell me, "Clean up before you come in." He offered, "Come in and I'll clean you up." It's not my grip on him that matters but his grip on me. And his grip is sure.

Because of Bethlehem, I have a Savior in heaven. Christmas begins what Easter celebrates. The child in the cradle became the King on the cross.

So is his presence in my life. Christmas presents from Santa? That's nice. But the perpetual presence of Christ? That's life changing.

God is always near us. Always for us. Always in us. We may forget him, but God will never forget us. We are forever on his mind and in his plans. He called himself "'Immanuel' (which means 'God with us')" (Matt. 1:23).

Not just "God made us."

Not just "God thinks of us."

Not just "God above us."

But God *with* us. God where we are: at the office, in the kitchen, on the plane. He breathed our air and walked this earth. God . . . with . . . us!

We need this message more than ever. We live in anxious times. Terrorism is living up to its name—terror. Violence hangs over our planet like a dark cloud. Think about the images on the news: the senseless attacks, the bloodshed, the random acts of cruelty.

And, as if the malice were inadequate, there is the fear of another recession. We seem to teeter on the edge of bull markets going bear and the financial world going down. The shepherds stayed awake, watching their flocks by night. You've been sleeping with one eye open trying to keep watch over your stocks by night.

And there is more:

The job you can't keep
The tumor you can't diagnose
The marriage you can't fix
The boss you can't please

We can relate to the little boy who played the part of the angel in the Christmas story. He and his mother rehearsed his lines over and over: "It is I; don't be afraid." "It is I; don't be afraid."

Yet, when the Christmas pageant began, he walked onto the stage and saw the lights and audience and he froze. After an awkward silence, he finally said, "It is me and I'm scared."

Are you scared? If so, may I suggest that you need a little Christmas? I don't mean a dose of saccharine sentiment or Santa cheer or double-spiked eggnog. That's not Christmas.

Christmas, as my dad said, is about Christ. Christ's name occupies six of the nine letters, for crying out loud. This isn't Santa-mas, or shopping-mas, or reindeer-mas. This is *Christ*-mas. And *Christ*-mas is not *Christ*-mas unless or until you receive the message of Bethlehem.

God is always near us. Always for us. Always in us. We may forget him, but God will never forget us.

Have you? In the hurry and scurry of the season, have you taken time to receive the promise of the season?

- God gets us.
- God saves us.

God is always near us. By the way, Bethlehem was just the beginning. Jesus has promised a repeat performance. Bethlehem, Act 2. No silent night this time, however. The skies will open, trumpets will blast, and a new kingdom will begin. He will empty the tombs and melt the winter of death. He will press his thumb against the collective cheek of his children and wipe away all tears. "Begone, sorrow, sickness, wheelchairs, and cancer! Enough of you, screams of fear and nights of horror! Death, you die! Life, you reign!" The manger invites, even dares us to believe the best is yet to be. And it could all begin today.

But if it doesn't, there is a reason. No day is accidental or incidental. No acts are random or wasted. Look at the Bethlehem birth. A king ordered a census. Joseph was forced to travel. Mary, as round as a ladybug, bounced on a donkey's back. The hotel was full. The hour was late. The event was one big hassle. Yet, out of the hassle, hope was born.

It still is. I don't like hassles. But I love Christmas because it reminds us how "God causes everything to work together for the good of those who love God" (Rom. 8:28 NLT).

The heart-shaping promises of Christmas. Long after the guests have left and the carolers have gone home and the lights have come down, these promises endure.

Perhaps you could use some Christmas this Christmas?

Let's do what I did as a six-year-old, redheaded, flat-topped, freckle-faced boy. Let's turn on the lamp, curl up in a comfortable spot, and look into the odd, wonderful story of Bethlehem.

May you find what I have found: a lifetime of hope.

2

God Has a Face

hy do we punch elevator buttons more than once?

Why do we love the front seat of a bus and the backseat of a church?

Why do we pierce holes in our bodies and hang jewelry from them?

Why do we ask for instructions and then argue with the person who gave them?

Of what purpose is a necktie?

Rational behavior is not one of our trademarks. But if you want to see people on the edge of insanity, just watch the way families treat their babies at Christmastime.

The poor child has no warning. He is just starting to recover from the slide down the birth canal when the family begins decorating him as if he were a puppy in the dog parade. Red furry stocking cap with a white ball on the end. Goofy elfish shoes that curl at the toes. When this baby becomes a teen and wears baggy jeans and sports a tattoo, grown-ups will groan at the sight. But dress a six-month-old in suspenders and reindeer antlers? That's cute.

And the gifts we give. The little one can't get out of her crib, yet ever-earnest Mommy has her hooked on phonics. He can't even walk without help, and Grandpa gives him a Louisville Slugger baseball bat.

And the pictures we take!

Baby teething on the ornaments
Baby snoozing under the tree
Baby on Santa's lap
Santa with wet spot on lap

We make such a fuss! Bring the baby into a room, and everything changes. Grandma reaches up. Grandpa wakes up. Conversation shifts from politics and presidents to Pampers and pacifiers. This time of year babies take center stage. And well they should. Is not Christmas the story of a baby?

Heaven's seed enwombed in Mary.
Minuscule, yet mighty.
A fetus, yet a force.
God descends a birth canal.
Born.
Creator cradled in a Bethlehem barn.
Infant, yet infinite.
Asleep, yet a King.

God gurgles in Mama's arms.
Baby.

This is the Christmas moment that shaped all the others to follow. On a starlit night in the company of sheep, cattle, and a bewildered Joseph, Mary's eyes fell upon the face of her just-born son. She was bone weary, surely. In pain, likely. Ready to place her head on the straw and sleep the rest of the night away, probably. But first Mary had to see this face. *His* face. To wipe the moisture from his mouth and feel the shape of his chin. To be the first to whisper, "So this is what God looks like."

―――∞∞∞―――

Jesus entered our world not *like* a human but *as* a human.

―――∞∞∞―――

People have always wondered about the image of God. Societies have speculated. Tribes have cogitated. And we've reached a variety of conclusions. God has been depicted as a golden calf and a violent wind and an angry volcano. He wears wings, breathes fire, eats infants, and demands penance. We've fancied God as ferocious, magical, fickle, and maniacal. A god to be avoided, dreaded, and appeased. But never in mankind's wildest imaginings did we consider that God would enter the world as an infant.

"The Word became flesh and dwelt among us" (John 1:14 NKJV). The Word became not a whirlwind or a devouring fire but a single cell, a fertilized egg, an embryo—a baby. Placenta nourished him. An amniotic sac surrounded him. He grew to the size of a fist. His tiny heart divided into chambers. God became flesh.

Jesus entered our world not *like* a human but *as* a human. He endured puberty, pimples, hot weather, and cranky neighbors. God became human down to his very toes. He had suspended the stars and ladled out the seas, yet he suckled a breast and slept in hay.

Some years ago I wrote a chapter titled "Twenty-Five Questions for Mary," in which I imagined the ponderings that young Mary had about Jesus.[1] The idea captured the imagination of an elementary-school teacher. She asked her students to make a list of questions they would have liked to ask young Mary. Here are some of their responses:

"Could you believe that you were pregnant for the whole world?"

"Were you scared of not doing a good job?"

"What was Jesus' first word as a baby?"

"Was he beautiful?"

"Did he ever get sick?"

"Did Jesus ever misbehave?"

"Was Jesus born with hair?"

"What was his favorite food?"

"Did you feel any holier?"

"Did he ever have a pet?"

These are legitimate questions. The fact that we can ask them raises a greater one.

Why such a journey? Why did God go so far?

> Why did God go so far? He wants you to know that he gets you. He understands how you feel and has faced what you face.

A chief reason is this: he wants you to know that he gets you. He understands how you feel and has faced what you face. Jesus is not "out of touch with our reality. He's been through weakness and testing, experienced it all—all but the sin. So let's walk right up to him and get what he is so ready to give. Take the mercy, accept the help" (Heb. 4:15–16 MSG).

Since you know he understands, you can boldly go to him. Because of Bethlehem's miracle, you can answer these fundamental questions: Does God care if I'm sad? Look at the tear-streaked face of Jesus as he stands near Lazarus's tomb. Does God notice when I'm afraid? Note the resolve in the eyes of Jesus as he marches through the storm to rescue his friends. Does God know if I am ignored or rejected?

Find the answer in the compassionate eyes of Christ as he stands to defend the adulterous woman.[2]

"[Jesus] radiates God's own glory and expresses the very character of God" (Heb. 1:3 NLT). Jesus himself stated, "Anyone who has seen me has seen the Father" (John 14:9).

"Anyone who has seen me weep has seen the Father weep."

"Anyone who has seen me laugh has seen the Father laugh."

"Anyone who has seen me determined has seen the Father determined."

Would you like to see God? Take a look at Jesus.

In 1926 George Harley founded a medical mission among the Mano tribe of Liberia. The locals were receptive to the doctor and helped him construct a clinic and a chapel. Eventually Harley treated more than ten thousand patients a year. During the first five years, however, not one person from the tribe visited his chapel.

Shortly after the doctor and his wife arrived, she gave birth to Robert, their first child. The boy grew up on the edge of the forest. "He was the apple of our eye," Harley later said. "How we loved our little boy! But one day when he was almost five years old, I looked out the window of the medical dispensary and saw Bobby. He was running across the field but he fell down. Then he got up and ran some more and fell again. But this time he didn't get up. So I ran out and picked up the feverish body of my own little boy.

I held him in my arms and said, 'Bobby, don't worry. Your daddy knows how to treat that tropical fever. He's going to help you get better.'"

Dr. Harley tried every treatment he knew. But nothing helped. The fever raged, and in short order the disease took the boy's life. The parents were distraught with grief. The missionary went into his workshop and built a coffin. Harley placed Robert inside and nailed the lid. He lifted the coffin on his shoulder and walked toward the clearing to find a place to dig a grave. One of the old men in the village saw him and asked about the box. When Harley explained that his son had died, the old man offered to help him carry the coffin. Dr. Harley told a friend what happened next:

> So the old man took one end of the coffin and I took the other. Eventually we came to the clearing in the forest. We dug a grave there and laid Bobby in it. But when we had covered up the grave, I just couldn't stand it any longer . . . I fell down on my knees in the dirt and began to sob uncontrollably. My beloved son was dead, and there I was in the middle of an African jungle 8,000 miles from home and relatives. I felt so all alone.
>
> But when I started crying, the old man cocked his head in stunned amazement. He squatted down beside me and looked at me so intently. For a long time, he sat there listening to me cry. Then suddenly, he leaped to his feet and went running back up the trail through

the jungle, screaming, again and again, at the top of his voice, "White man, white man—he cries like one of us."[3]

That evening as Harley and his wife grieved in their cottage, there was a knock at the door. Harley opened it. There stood the chief and almost every man, woman, and child in the village. They were back again the next Sunday and filled the chapel to overflowing. They wanted to hear about Jesus.

Everything changed when the villagers saw the tears of the missionary.

Everything changes when we see the face of God.

He took on your face in the hope that you would see his.

He came with tears too. He knows the burden of a broken heart. He knows the sorrow this life can bring. He could have come as a shining light or a voice in the clouds, but he came as a person. Does God understand you? Find the answer in Bethlehem.

Gaze where Mary gazed. Look into God's face and be assured. If the King was willing to enter the world of animals and shepherds and swaddling clothes, don't you think he's willing to enter yours?

He took on your face in the hope that you would see his.

3

Saved from Ourselves

I tried to blame my behavior on the holiday traffic. The Thanksgiving weekend had turned the streets near the shopping mall into controlled chaos.

I tried to blame my misdeeds on my state of mind. I was driving to my in-laws' house, having spent most of the day helping to plan a funeral for Denalyn's ever-weakening mother.

I tried to blame my poor reaction on the reckless U-turn made by the teenager. He nearly clipped my bumper.

The traffic arrow invited me to make a right turn into the busy avenue. As I did, the teenager made a sudden, unexpected hairpin turn around the median. We nearly shared paint. I honked at him. I'll confess: my honk wasn't a polite "Ahem, excuse me. I am over here." It was long and strong and demanded, "Do you know what you almost did?"

He drove a low-riding, wide-wheeled, two-toned, exhaust-puffing jalopy that dated back to the eighties. It needed a muffler. It also needed a more mature passenger. As the car accelerated, a long arm came out of the passenger-side window and gave me a backhanded, one-fingered wave.

Grrr. I sped up.

Thanks to a traffic light I was soon side by side with the perpetrator. He still had his window down. I lowered mine. He looked up at me. He wore a baseball cap shoved over a mop of black hair. The brim of the cap faced sideways. So did the smirk on his face.

"You need to watch that wave, son."

In an ideal world he would have apologized, and I would have wished him a merry Christmas, and I wouldn't be telling you this story.

But the world is not ideal. When I told him to "watch that wave," he smirked even more and demanded, "Make me!"

Make me? When was the last time I heard someone say, "Make me"? Middle school? High school locker room? There was that scuffle after the graduation party. *Make me?* That's what teens say. Of course, he was a teen. He didn't have a whisker on him. He was a skinny, floppy-haired, testosterone-laden adolescent who was feeling his oats riding shotgun in his buddy's muscle car.

As for me, I am a sixty-year-old pastor who writes Christian books and speaks at conferences and feels a call to make the world a better place. I should have raised my window. But I didn't. I looked down at him, literally and metaphorically, and said with my own version of a smirk, "Now, what did you say?"

"Make me," he repeated.

The saints in heaven were saying, "Drive away, Lucado."

Common sense was urging, "Drive away, Lucado."

The better angels of the universe were prompting, "Drive away, Lucado."

I didn't listen. The dare of the punk activated the punk inside me, the punk I hadn't seen in decades. I snarled. "Okay, where do you want to go?"

His eyes widened to the size of hamburger patties. He couldn't believe I'd said that. I couldn't believe I'd said that. You can't believe I said that. When he realized I was serious, he became the same.

"Let's settle this at the shopping mall."

"Are you kidding?" I told him. "There are too many people in a shopping mall. Follow me." Whaaat? All of a sudden I was the expert on where to go to duke it out?

The light turned and I accelerated. In my side-view mirror I could see that the two boys were engaged in a heated exchange.

"What do you think?"

"I dunno. What do you think?"

"He looks pretty cranky."

"Yeah, he might have a weapon or sump'n."

By the time I reached the next stoplight, they were nowhere to be seen. They must have turned into the parking lot.

Boy, was I relieved. I drove the rest of the way to my

in-laws' house, asking myself, *Did you really just dare a kid to fight? Are you crazy?*

I'd like to blame my behavior on my state of mind, the stress of the traffic, the driver who nearly hit my car, or the passenger who pushed my buttons. But I can blame my bizarre behavior on only one thing. The punk inside me. For a few minutes at a stoplight near a shopping mall, I forgot who I was.

And I forgot who the teenager was. In that heated moment he wasn't someone's son. He wasn't a creation of God. He wasn't a miracle. He wasn't fearfully and wonderfully made. He was a disrespectful jerk, and I let him bring out the disrespectful jerk in me.

The Bible has a name for this punkish tendency—sin. The sinful nature is the stubborn, self-centered attitude that says, "My way or the highway." The sinful nature is all about self: pleasing self, promoting self, preserving self. Sin is selfish.

I have a sin nature.

So do you. (Merry Christmas.) Under the right circumstances you will do the wrong thing. You won't want to. You'll try not to, but you will. Why? You have a sin nature.

You were born with it. We all were. Our parents didn't teach us to throw temper tantrums; we were born with the skill. No one showed us how to steal a cookie from our sibling; we just knew. We never attended a class on pouting or passing the blame, but we could do both before we were out of our diapers. The heart of the human problem is the problem of the human heart.

—— ❦ ——

The heart of the human problem is the problem of the human heart.

—— ❦ ——

Each one of us entered the world with a sin nature. God entered the world to take it away. Christmas commemorates the day and the way God saved us from ourselves. Look carefully at the words the angel spoke to Joseph.

Joseph son of David, do not be afraid to take Mary home as your wife, because what is conceived in her is from the Holy Spirit. She will give birth to a son, and you are to give him the name Jesus, because he will save his people from their sins. (Matt. 1:20–21)

We may not see the connection between the name *Jesus* and the phrase "save his people from their sins," but Joseph would have. He was familiar with the Hebrew language. The English name *Jesus* traces its origin to the Hebrew word *Yeshua*. *Yeshua* is a shortening of *Yehoshuah*, which means "Yahweh saves."[1]

Who was Jesus? *God* saves.

What did Jesus come to do? God *saves*.

God saves. Jesus was not just godly, godlike, God hungry, God focused, or God worshipping. He was God. Not merely a servant of God, instrument of God, or friend of God, but Jesus was God.

God *saves*, not God empathizes, cares, listens, helps, assists, or applauds. God saves. Specifically "he will save his people from their sins" (v. 21). Jesus came to save us, not just from politics, enemies, challenges, or difficulties. He came to save us from our own sins.

Jesus came to save us, not just from politics, enemies, challenges, or difficulties. He came to save us from our own sins.

Here's why. God has high plans for you and me. He is recruiting for himself a people who will populate heaven. God will restore his planet and his children to their garden of Eden splendor. It will be perfect. Perfect in splendor. Perfect in righteousness. Perfect in harmony.

One word describes heaven: *perfect*.

One word describes us: *imperfect*.

God's kingdom is perfect, but his children are not, so what is he to do? Abandon us? Start over? He could. But he loves us too much to do that.

Will he tolerate us with our sin nature? Populate heaven with rebellious, self-centered citizens? If so, how would heaven be heaven?

He had a greater plan. "God was pleased for all of himself to live in Christ" (Col. 1:19 NCV).

All the love of God was in Jesus. All the strength of God was in Jesus. All the compassion and power and devotion of God were, for a time, in the earthly body of a carpenter.

No wonder the winds obeyed when Jesus spoke; he was *God speaking*.

No wonder the bacteria fled when Jesus touched the wounds; he was *God touching*.

No wonder the water held him as he walked; he was *God walking*.

No wonder the people stood speechless as he taught; he was *God teaching*.

And no wonder ten thousand angels stood in rapt attention as Jesus was nailed to the cross; he was *God dying*.

He let people crucify him, for goodness' sake! He became sin for our sake. "He made Him who knew no sin to be sin for us" (2 Cor. 5:21 NKJV). What started in the Bethlehem cradle culminated on the Jerusalem cross.

But that's not all.

Jesus not only did a work *for* us; he does a work *within*

us. "The mystery in a nutshell is just this: Christ is in you" (Col. 1:27 MSG).

He commandeers our hands and feet, requisitions our minds and tongues. "He decided from the outset to shape the lives of those who love him along the same lines as the life of his Son" (Rom. 8:29 MSG).

Having paid sin's penalty, Christ defuses sin's power. The punk within diminishes, and the Christ within flourishes. God changes us day by day from one level to the next. We'll never be sinless, but we will sin less.

We'll never be sinless,
but we will sin less.

And when we do sin, we have this assurance: the grace that saved us also preserves us. We may lose our tempers, our perspective, and our self-control. But we never lose our hope. Why? Because God has his hold on us. He "is able to keep you from stumbling, and to present you faultless before the presence of His glory with exceeding joy" (Jude v. 24 NKJV).

The believer has been saved from the guilt of sin, is being saved from problems of sin, and, upon the return of Christ, will be saved from the punishment for sin. Complete and full-service salvation.

God saves!

And *only* God saves. If we could save ourselves, why would we need a Savior? Jesus did not enter the world to help us save ourselves. He entered the world to save us from ourselves.

As a Boy Scout, I earned a lifesaving merit badge. I never actually saved anyone. In fact, the only people I saved were other Boy Scouts who didn't need to be saved. During training I would rescue other trainees. We took turns saving each other. But since we weren't really drowning, we resisted being rescued.

"Stop kicking and let me save you," I'd say.

It's impossible to save those who are trying to save themselves.

You might save yourself from a broken heart or going broke or running out of gas. But you aren't good enough to save yourself from sin. You aren't strong enough to save yourself from death. You need a Savior.

Because of Bethlehem you have one.

———— ∞ ————

You need a Savior. Because of
Bethlehem you have one.

———— ∞ ————

When you say yes to him, he says yes to you. He will change your sin nature into his nature. Good to know, especially in holiday traffic.

If perchance these words find their way to a couple of brash kids who recognize this story, to you I say, "I'm sorry. Your actions were wrong, but my reaction was worse. God is working on us all."

4

Hope for the Hole-idays

*C*hristmas is a season of interruptions. Some we enjoy. Some we don't.

We enjoy interrupting diets for eggnog, work for a staff party, and bill paying for Christmas cards.

But we could do without the Chicago snowstorm that grounds the Atlanta flight, which strands the passengers in Albuquerque. We could do without the midnight phone call from Cousin Bert saying that he and Mary Lou and their kids are going to be in the area for the holidays. Could they park their Winnebago in the driveway for "Oh, we promise, no more than ten days"?

Interruptions. They come with Christmas. They come with life.

Just when you sell the crib—surprise! Another child. Just when you're ready to retire—surprise! More tuition. Just when you thought your plans were finalized—surprise! More layoffs, surgery, transfers, or treatments.

Interruptions. They can stir fear and anxiety. They steal

our sleep and pickpocket our joy. They can cause us to question God, even turn away from God.

You may be facing an interruption in this season of life. What you wanted and what you received do not match. And now you are troubled and anxious, even angry. Does that describe you?

It certainly described our family last Christmas.

It was the second weekend of the Advent season. I'd spent the day preparing for and speaking at a Saturday night church service. By the time I arrived home, it was well into the evening hours. Denalyn was waiting for me in the kitchen. I could tell by her expression that something was wrong.

"Max, Jenna is pregnant."

Her announcement did not match her demeanor. Denalyn should have been waving her arms and hugging me. Grandparents at last! But there was no confetti, just concern. Her eyes were tear filled.

"She's in the emergency room."

We raced to the hospital.

Emergency rooms do not wear Christmas decorations well. A garland does not make an X-ray machine festive. Red and green bulbs cannot shed a happy glow on a gurney. No matter the song on the intercom, the monitors beep louder than the sleigh bells ring. An ER is still an ER. Even at Christmas. And our daughter was in the ER.

A nurse led us down the hallway into a room. Jenna

was on the bed. She tried to be stoic and succeeded, for about ten seconds. Then she began to cry. She had wanted to surprise the family. She wanted to make a big deal out of a Christmas pregnancy. She wanted to have a baby.

By the end of the night, we knew that wasn't likely.

By the next morning the doctor assured us it wasn't to be.

It had already been a tough season for Jenna and her husband, Brett. His dad had died a month earlier. Their November was gray with sorrow. Now December was going to be even more so.

Jenna said her Christmas felt more like a hole-iday than a holiday.

Maybe yours feels the same. More tear than cheer. More yuck than yule.

- The sight of happy children is a reminder of a vacant crib.
- The busy social schedule of some only highlights your empty one.
- Images of families together reinforce your pain of a family apart.

If this season is hard for you, if you're looking forward to December 26 more than December 25, then I have a story for you to consider. A story of a young girl.

As much as she tried to keep a good attitude, it was not

easy. She was far from home, miles from family and her own bed. She had spent the last few days on crowded roads, enduring the winter chill. Money was scarce. Friends were nowhere near. A warm bed and a hot meal? The prospects were slim.

Ask her which was worse, the pain in her heart or the pain in her back, and she'd be hard pressed to make a choice.

Her heart ached for her family. She felt estranged from them. Under normal circumstances they would have been thrilled to learn of her pregnancy. But pregnant before the wedding? With her conservative family and her bizarre explanation? And to have to tell the man she was to marry that she was carrying a child who wasn't his? It was a miracle he still married her. And another miracle was what she needed that night.

She'd envisioned giving birth at home: Mom holding one hand, an aunt the other; a midwife, doting relatives, Joseph, and a crowd of neighbors outside the door. Perhaps if they all could have experienced the birth of her firstborn together, then they would believe her story.

At least that's how I imagine Mary felt. Of course, I could be wrong. Perhaps the feed trough and stable were her idea. But I don't think so. I've yet to meet a mother-to-be who dreams of using a cow stall for a delivery room and a manger for a bassinet. I doubt Mary did either. So when Joseph returned from the inn and asked if she was allergic to sheep, it's a safe hunch to say she was chagrined. This wasn't how she had planned to celebrate the birth of Jesus.

Joseph led the donkey down a steep path that ended at the mouth of a cave carved out years before by the wind and the rain, used as long as anyone could remember for a barn. He lowered Mary off the back of the donkey. He looked at her face, fatigued and powdery from the road. He apologized for the austere accommodations. She touched his cheek and smiled and entered the grotto.

Joseph built a fire and heated water. Mary cleared a spot on the straw and set about the task of bringing God into the world. With cows as her witnesses and Joseph as her midwife, she did just that.

Within moments the hand of the Star Hanger clutched Mary's finger. The feet of the Sky Walker lay in Joseph's palm. No wonder the angels filled the sky with worship. Any doubt of the Father's love disappeared the night God was wrapped in barnyard towels so the hay wouldn't scratch his back.

Any doubt of the Father's love disappeared the night God was wrapped in barnyard towels so the hay wouldn't scratch his back.

In that moment Mary knew it was all worth it. The ache in her back, the ache in her heart—they faded away. The questions of how, the wonderings of when—they didn't linger. The inn had no place for her son; that was all right. He would find a place in people's hearts. She and Joseph were far from home on the night of Jesus' birth; that was all right. Jesus was even farther from his. There was no warm bed in which Jesus could sleep? No problem.

In spite of the chaos, Christ came.

Through a scandalous pregnancy, an imposed census, an untimely trip, and an overcrowded inn, God triumphed in Mary's story.

And he triumphed in Matthew's genealogy. We don't often mention the lineage of Jesus in context with his birth. Matthew did, however. He opens his gospel with a list with dozens of names. Before he presents the wise men and the star of Bethlehem, he tells us that "Abraham begot Isaac, Isaac begot Jacob, and Jacob begot Judah and his brothers. Judah begot Perez and Zerah by Tamar, Perez begot Hezron, and Hezron begot Ram" (Matt. 1:2–3 NKJV).

The list goes on and on (and on) for sixteen verses. "Obed begot Jesse, and Jesse begot David the king. David the king begot Solomon" (vv. 5–6 NKJV). *Yawn.* Let's skip to the nativity story! Who needs to know about Tamar, Rahab, and Ruth? Why does Matthew mention David and Solomon before he mentions Joseph and Mary?

He is making a point. Chaos cannot keep Christ out of his world. The Messiah was born not because of his ancestors but in spite of them. Tamar was abandoned. Ruth was an immigrant, and Rahab was a harlot. David was an adulterer. Solomon was a philanderer. The family tree of Jesus is gnarled and crooked. Some of the kings were blood-thirsty and godless. Yet God had promised that Jesus would come, and Jesus came. Hence the triumphant conclusion of the genealogy:

> Jacob was the father of Joseph, who married a woman named Mary. It was Mary who gave birth to Jesus, and it is Jesus who is the Savior, the Anointed One. (v. 16 *The Voice*)

Christ came!
In spite of sin and scandal, Christ came.
In spite of racism and sexism, Christ came.
Though the people forgot God, Christ came.
In spite of, and out of, the pandemonium, Christ came.
The surprise pregnancy, the sudden census, the long road from Nazareth to Bethlehem. Unpleasant and difficult, yet they resulted in the world's greatest miracle. "And [Mary] brought forth her firstborn Son, and wrapped Him in swaddling cloths, and laid Him in a manger" (Luke 2:7 NKJV). Everything before this happened so this moment would happen. Was the first Christmas different from what Mary had planned? Yes, but it turned out greater than she could have dreamed. God used the struggles to accomplish his will.

Don't you need that reminder? In your world of short

nights, hard work, and high stress, don't you need to know that Jesus holds it all together?

You might relate to the jalopy I once saw. The car clattered down the freeway, one door missing, hood dented, needing paint. On the loosely hanging bumper was this sticker: "Honk if anything falls off."

"For everything, absolutely everything, above and below, visible and invisible, rank after rank after rank of angels—*everything* got started in him and finds its purpose in him. He was there before any of it came into existence and holds it all together right up to this moment" (Col. 1:16–17 MSG).

You cannot face a crisis if you
don't face God first.

God holds it all together. And he will hold it together for you.

Everything inside you and every voice around you says, "Get out. Get angry. Get drunk. Get high." But don't listen to the voices. You cannot face a crisis if you don't face God first.

> Don't worry about anything; instead, pray about everything; tell God your needs, and don't forget to thank him for his answers. If you do this,

you will experience God's peace, which is far more
wonderful than the human mind can understand.
His peace will keep your thoughts and your hearts
quiet and at rest as you trust in Christ Jesus. (Phil.
4:6–7 TLB)

Cling to him. In the ER, when your dreams are falling apart, say to him, "Lord, I need you now." Between
the headstones of the cemetery, whisper, "Dear Jesus, lift
me up." During the deposition, when others are grumbling
beneath their breath, may you be overheard repeating this
prayer: "God, you are good. I . . . need . . . help. Encourage
me, please."

In the prayer journal of King David, we read this question: "When all that is good falls apart, what can good
people do?" (Ps. 11:3 NCV).

Isn't David's question ours? When all that is good falls
apart, what can good people do?

When terrorists attack, when diseases rage, when families collapse, when churches divide . . . when all that is good
falls apart, what can good people do? What is the godly
response to the unexpected mishaps and calamities of life?

Curiously, David didn't answer his question with an
answer. He answered it with a declaration. "The LORD is
in his holy temple. The LORD is on his throne in heaven"
(v. 4 NIrV).

His point is unmistakable: When everything shakes,

God remains unshaken. He is in his holy temple. His plan will not be derailed. God is unaffected by our storms. He is undeterred by our problems.

———⊗⊗⊗———

When everything shakes, God remains unshaken.

———⊗⊗⊗———

Remember the story of Jacob's son Joseph in Egypt? Look at him in the prison. His brothers sold him out; Potiphar's wife turned him in. If ever a world caved in, Joseph's did.

Or consider Moses, watching flocks in the wilderness. Was this what he intended to do with his life? Hardly. His heart beat with Jewish blood. His passion was to lead the slaves, so why did God have him leading sheep?

And Daniel? He was among the brightest and best young men of Israel—the equivalent of a West Point Cadet or Ivy Leaguer. But he and his entire generation were being marched out of Jerusalem into Babylonian captivity. The city was destroyed. The temple was in ruins.

Joseph in prison. Moses in the desert. Daniel in chains. These were dark moments. Who could have seen any good in them? Who could have known that Joseph the prisoner was just one promotion from becoming Joseph the prime minister? Who would have thought that God was giving Moses forty years of wilderness training in the very desert through which he would lead the people? And who could have imagined that Daniel, the captive, would soon be Daniel the king's counselor?

God has made a business out of turning tragedy into triumph. He did with Joseph, with Moses, with Daniel, and, most of all, he did with Jesus on the cross. The innocent one was slaughtered. Heaven's gift was murdered. Mothers wept, evil danced, and the apostles had to wonder, "When all that is good falls apart, what do good people do?"

God answered their question with a declaration, with the rumble of the earth and the rolling of the rock. He reminded them, "The LORD is in his holy temple. The LORD is on his throne in heaven" (Ps. 11:4 NIrv).

Is your Christmas a difficult one? Then take heart. God is still in his temple, still on his throne, still in control. And he still makes princes out of prisoners, counselors out of captives, Sundays out of Fridays, and he still brings beauty out of Bethlehems.

He did then, for them. He does it still, for you and me.

5

It's Never Too Late

The gift is hidden in my sock drawer. It's nestled in the back right corner between the blacks and the browns. Denalyn will open the box on Christmas morning. The room will fill with the sound of oohs and aahs. She will clasp the chain around her neck and display the pendant and smile at her husband. One of our daughters will exclaim, "What a perfect gift!" Another will ask, "Dad, how did you know?"

It was easy. I took the hint. When Denalyn made her Christmas wishes known, I took her wishes home and hid them in my sock drawer. I'll get great reviews. But the truth? Denalyn all but bought her gift.

She escorted me into the mall jewelry store and asked the salesclerk to pull the pendant out of the glass counter. She held the chain against her neck and examined the medallion in the mirror on the counter. She then spoke to me, pacing her speech as one might with a non-English speaker. "Max . . . I . . . like . . . this . . ."

The woman behind the counter joined in. "I think your

wife likes this necklace, product number 251, in case you ever need to know."

"Max, are you listening?"

I wasn't. I was gazing out at the foot traffic, noting the large number of people wearing football jerseys, which reminded me of Sunday's big game, a must-win for the Dallas Cowboys if they were going to make the play-offs. That thought prompted a mental review of my calendar. *Will I be home for the game? Do we have snacks? I love to eat barbecue potato chips during a game. In fact, I'd love some right now. Does anyone in this mall sell them?*

"Max." The voice came from a distant place.

"Max." It sounded familiar.

"Max!" That's when I remembered where I was. (I never got the chips.)

I turned. Denalyn was looking at me. The salesclerk was looking at me. I had a feeling that every female in sight was looking at me. Hints began dropping like snow in a Winnipeg winter.

Denalyn to me: "Christmas is next month, Max."

Salesclerk: "You can pick this up at any point, Mr. Lucado."

Denalyn to salesclerk: "What was the product number again?"

Salesclerk to Denalyn: "Number 251."

Denalyn to me: "Let me write that down just in

case someone I married needs help with his shopping list."

Salesclerk to me: "We are open until 9:00 p.m."

Denalyn to me: "They are open until 9:00 p.m."

I just nodded and smiled. Truth be told, I need all the nudges I can get. If only every decision in life were this easy. All I did was pay attention.

Oh, that the same could be said about the innkeeper. He could have witnessed the birth of Jesus. All he needed to do was make room for the couple from Nazareth. But he didn't. And because he didn't, Scripture contains these sad lines:

> While they were in Bethlehem, the time came for Mary to have the baby, and she gave birth to her first son. Because there were no rooms left in the inn, she wrapped the baby with pieces of cloth and laid him in a feeding trough. (Luke 2:6–7 NCV)

So much is left unsaid in this passage. We know nothing about the innkeeper or the inn or the time of day. What we do know is this: he did not invite them in. There was no vacancy. The census turned sleepy Bethlehem into a boom-town. The innkeeper filled every room and closet. He placed someone in every bed, an occupant in every cot. He lined the hallways with mats and rollaways. The place was crowded.

But, honestly, couldn't he have found one more space? Mary was third-trimester pregnant. Wouldn't you find a bed for a mother-to-be? Of course you would. Which makes me wonder, was there another reason Jesus' parents were turned away?

Maybe the knock on the door was at midnight. The last candle had been snuffed out, the last dish washed. The only sound was the popping of the fireplace coals and the snoring of the slumbering guests. The innkeeper answered the door wearing his nightshirt. Through a six-inch opening he peered into the dark and told Joseph, "It's too late. We're all bedded down. Earlier there might have been room. Earlier I might have made room. But at this hour? I'm sorry."

Besides, Mary's pregnancy might prove problematic. What if she screamed during labor and woke up the other guests? And the baby? Babies can be noisy, restless. This was a hotel, not a maternity ward.

Perhaps the hour was too late.

Or the couple was too common.

Simple villagers, they were. Hoi polloi. Had Mary and Joseph been Queen Mary and King Joseph, the innkeeper would have responded differently. Had they arrived with camels and servants instead of a few clothes and a tired donkey—had they been uncommon—the response of the innkeeper might have been uncommon. But no trumpet sounded. No herald proclaimed. No courier announced their arrival. There was only a knock.

A knock at the door . . .
    by a common couple . . .
        at a late hour . . .
            when the inn was crowded.
So the innkeeper missed the opportunity.

———— ✸ ————

The innkeeper missed the opportunity. Many still do.

———— ✸ ————

Many still do. They miss the chance to open the door. They let the birth of Jesus pass them by. The miracle of Bethlehem still happens. God enters the hamlets of our lives and speaks to us. He speaks through scriptures, sunsets, the kindness of a friend, or the warning of a medical report. He sings to us through Christmas carols. He calls to us through Christmas sermons. He reaches out through the Christmas story.

"Here I am!" Jesus invites. "I stand at the door and knock. If you hear my voice and open the door, I will come in and eat with you, and you will eat with me" (Rev. 3:20 NCV).

I have a friend who works with churches in Papua New Guinea. Many in their culture don't knock on doors. They stand at the doorframe and politely cough to announce their presence. When Bible translators tried to explain the idea of Jesus knocking on the door, it made no sense to the locals.

The missionaries solved the cross-cultural problem by rendering the verse "I stand at the door and cough."

Whether Jesus is clearing his throat or tapping on the door, the point is the same. He is gentle and polite. He never forces his way in. Yet just as we reach to open the door, the baby cries, the phone rings, the timer goes off, or the beep on the automated calendar reminds us to study for the exam, call the doctor, do the laundry, or cut the grass.

Life is crowded. Your life is crowded. Heaven knows, you already have more than you can do. And because heaven knows, Jesus comes not with a list of things for you to do but with a list of things he has already done and will do. Your death? Defeated. Your sins? Forgiven. Your fears? He will give you courage. Your questions? He will guide you.

Jesus lifts burdens; he doesn't add to them.

Jesus comes not with a list of things
for you to do but with a list of things
he has already done and will do. Jesus
lifts burdens; he doesn't add to them.

"But it's too late," you say. No it isn't. It's never too late for Christ.

You are never too old, too messed up, or too worn-out. Elijah was depressed. God still came to him. Abraham was old. God still led him. Moses was long retired. God still called him. Jonah was on the run. God still used him. Jacob cheated his family. God still had a place for him. Peter betrayed Christ, Saul persecuted Christ, Thomas doubted Christ, but each learned it was not too late for Christ.

———— ∞ ————

It's never too late to come to Christ for help.

———— ∞ ————

I was called to the bedside of a dying man a few days back, an eighty-year-old scoundrel. Yes, a scoundrel! He spent the final decade of his life with time on his hands, money at his disposal, and women on his mind. His exploits would have made Hugh Hefner blush. But as his health began to fail, his conscience began to stir. When the doctor told him to get his affairs in order, he called me. He wanted to get right with God. He made a deathbed confession of faith.

Might I make a confession of my own? I left the hospital room with a scroogy scowl. *That's too easy*, I thought. *A guy like him deserves to be routed through purgatory on the way to paradise.*

But God didn't tell me to screen the applicants, just to teach them. And according to God's great grace, if my scoundrel friend's confession was sincere, he is walking the same heavenly streets as Paul and Peter and King David. Each a scoundrel in his own right.

It's never too late to come to Christ for help. Your stack of sins is never too high. Your list of failures is never too long. That knock at the door of your heart? That's Jesus.

It's one thing to miss a message from your spouse, but to miss a message from God? That's a mistake you don't want to make.

All you have to do is open the door.

6

Worship Works Wonders

Dear Ladies,

We know you mean well. We know you think you know best. But enough is enough. We have suffered in silence for too long. Having shared our pain with one another, we husbands hereby step out of the shadows and open our hearts. This year as you shop for our Christmas gifts, please don't buy us what we need.

We know we need to smell better and look nicer. We know you like us in warm pajamas and new underwear. But we do not know what to say when we open these gifts. How can you fake enthusiasm over house slippers? How can you look happy holding a nose-hair trimmer? We've lied long enough. For the sake of integrity on Christmas morning, we offer this guidance. As you look at any potential gift, ask yourself these questions: Can he play with it? Does it swing, bounce, shuffle, cast, or roll? Can you find a trigger, grip, rip cord, or stick shift? Does it consume oil or dog food? Does it have a big screen and a remote control? If it does, buy it. Doesn't matter that he already has one. This is no time to be practical.

When considering an item of men's apparel, ask your-self, is it brown and green and rain resistant? You can't lose with any garment that is. Realizing that many women prefer to shop anywhere but the gun department, we offer these two questions. Does it make him look cute? Does it make him look like a hunk? If the clothing makes him look cute, drop it immediately. If it makes him look like a hunk, buy two.

When all else fails, ask, can he eat it? Note, the question is not, would you eat it? Or do other humans eat it? Or is it edible? Don't occupy yourself with trivialities. The question is, can he eat it? Anytime the answer is affirmative, consider yourself on safe ground.

In closing we extend this offer. If you will buy us what we want, we will do the same for you. Without revealing any details we will tell you this. A large vacuum cleaner company has offered us a group discount. (And you thought we were insensitive.)

No need to thank us,
Your husbands

*C*hristmas and gift giving. The two have always been associated with each other for good reason. The magi gave Jesus the gifts of gold, frankincense, and myrrh. The shepherds gave Jesus the gift of their time and belief. Mary gave Jesus the gift of her womb. The offerings seem practical. The wise men's treasures could be used to fund the family's escape to Egypt. The shepherds' visitation would keep the family company. Mary's womb would protect the growing child. But there is one gift that might appear a bit curious.

The angels' gift of worship.

Suddenly, the angel was joined by a vast host of others—the armies of heaven—praising God:
"Glory to God in the highest heaven," they sang, "and peace on earth for all those pleasing him."
When this great army of angels had returned again to heaven, the shepherds said to each other, "Come on! Let's go to Bethlehem! Let's see this wonderful thing that has happened, which the Lord has told us about." (Luke 2:13–15 TLB)

The angels filled the night with light and the air with music, and, well, that's it. They worshipped. Couldn't they have done something more useful? Mary could have used a bed. Joseph would have benefited from an angelic escort back to Nazareth. Baby Jesus needed a bassinet.

These were angels. Didn't they know better?

Then again, these were angels. Who knew Jesus better than they? Those who knew Jesus best loved him dearest. Those who had followed him the longest gave him the gift of worship. They placed their love on a pillow of praise and presented it to Jesus. They did that night. They do so still. Heaven at this very moment reverberates with loud corporate worship. "Day and night they never stop saying: 'Holy, holy, holy'" (Rev. 4:8).

The word *worship* actually evolved from the Old English word *weorthscipe*. "To worship, then, is to ascribe worth to someone or something."[1]

Worship happens anytime you turn your heart toward heaven and say, "You are worthy." When you clear your calendar for prayer, turn the radio dial to praise music, or use your morning jog to recite Bible verses or your lunch break to meditate, this is worship.

Worship happens in neighborhoods, in living rooms, in open pastures. And, yes, worship happens in churches. When the people of God make a public and plural declaration of God's goodness, worship is happening.

God is on the hunt for those who will imitate the angels, for people who will open their hearts and mouths and declare, "Glory to God in the highest heaven." "The Father . . . is actively seeking such people to worship him" (John 4:23 NCV).

Perhaps you are wondering, *But what if I don't worship?*

Oh, but you will. The question is not, will you worship? The question is, where will you direct your worship? We all worship someone or something. Why, I once worshipped a bicycle!

At the age of eight I asked my parents to give me a bicycle for Christmas. Not just any bike but a fire-engine red Schwinn bike with a banana seat and high handlebars. They did! Basking in the light of the Christmas tree, it beckoned me to climb aboard and ride away into the bliss of childhood.

I decorated the handlebars with tassels and bought a reflector for the fender. I attached a playing card to the frame so it would *click, click, click* against the tire spokes. I was cool. James Dean–level cool. My bike and I explored subdivisions, drainage ditches, and dirt roads. I loved the bike. I *worshipped* the bike.

But then I wrecked it. I crashed into a curb and bent the frame. My dad and I tried to repair it, but the bike was never the same. It let me down. I was counting on it to carry me, to deliver me, to entertain me, to fulfill me. It didn't.

What about you? You were counting on that career to carry you, deliver you, entertain you, and fulfill you. But it hasn't.

You were counting on that marriage to carry you, deliver you, entertain you, and fulfill you. But it didn't.

You were counting on that retirement to carry you, deliver you, entertain you, and fulfill you. But it hasn't.

You were counting on that education to carry you, deliver you, entertain you, and fulfill you. But it didn't.

You were counting on that body to carry you, deliver you, entertain you, and fulfill you. But it hasn't.

Worship might not be the word you've used to describe your passion, yet the term fits. Anytime we trust an object or activity to give us life and meaning, we worship it.

When we make good things the ultimate things, we set ourselves up for disappointment.

When we make good things the ultimate things, we set ourselves up for disappointment. If we depend on a career or relationship to give our lives meaning, what happens when retirement comes or the relationship ends? The list of impostor gods includes sex, food, money, alcohol, success, and influence. In the correct dosage and context, these can be wonderful gifts from God. But they are dismal substitutes for God. To worship them is to be satisfied, then brokenhearted. Infatuated, then discouraged. Enthralled, then angry.

God-centered worship rescues us from bamboozlers, trompe l'oeil gods who never deliver on their promises. Worship does to the soul what a spring rain does to a thirsty field. It soaks down, seeps in, and stirs life. Are you stressed? Worship God, who could store the universe in his pocket and the oceans in an eyedropper. Are you ashamed? Worship Jesus, whose love never fades. Are you bereaved? Open your heart to your Shepherd. He will lead you through the valley of sorrow. Do you feel small? A few moments in front of the throne of your loving King will evaporate any sense of insignificance. Worship works wonders.

For your own sake do what the angels did: make a big deal about the arrival of the King.

For your own sake do what the angels did: make a big deal about the arrival of the King.

Worship verbally. "Through Jesus, therefore, let us continually offer to God a sacrifice of praise—the fruit of lips that openly profess his name" (Heb. 13:15).

In the early eighties there was a popular country song entitled "Always on My Mind."[2] The singer tells his sweetheart that even though he seldom expressed his feelings through words or actions, she was always on his mind. I'm not sure where the writer of those lyrics learned the secret of romance, but he didn't consult women. No sweetheart would accept that excuse. "You never told me, never gave me flowers, kind words, or compliments, but I was always on your mind? Yeah, right."

71

God doesn't buy it either. He wants to hear our affection. It is out of the abundance of the heart that the mouth speaks,[3] and when the mouth is silent, the heart is in question. Do you love God? Let him know. Tell him! Out loud. In public. Unashamed. Let there be jubilation, celebration, and festivity! "Shout to God with joyful praise!" (Ps. 47:1 NLT). "Make a joyful shout to God, all the earth!" (Ps. 66:1 NKJV).

John Wesley wrote, "Sing lustily, and with a good courage. Beware of singing as if you were half dead, or half asleep; but lift up your voice with strength. Be no more afraid of your voice now, nor more ashamed of its being heard, than when you sung the songs of Satan."[4]

Speaking of Satan, he cannot tolerate Christ-centered worship. Unlike God, he is not omniscient. Satan cannot read your mind. He is not moved by what you think, only by what you say. So say it! "Yell a loud *no* to the Devil and watch him scamper. Say a quiet *yes* to God and he'll be there in no time" (James 4:7–8 MSG). Do you want your city to be free from Satan's grip? Worship! Do you want your home to be loosed from the Devil? Worship! Do we want nations to be places of peace and prosperity? Then let the church assault Satan's strongholds with joy-filled praise. Worship verbally. And . . .

Worship in community. "There was . . . a *multitude* of the heavenly host praising God" (Luke 2:13 NKJV, emphasis mine). The presence of Christ deserves an abundant chorus. Every generation has its share of "Jesus, yes; church, no"

Christians. For a variety of reasons they turn away from church attendance. They do so at a great loss. Something happens in corporate worship that does not happen in private worship. When you see my face in the sanctuary and I hear your voice in the chorus, we are mutually edified. Granted, congregational worship is imperfect. We often sing off-key. Our attention tends to wander. The preacher stumbles over his words, and the organist misses her cue. Even so, let us worship. The sincerity of our worship matters more than the quality. "Let's see how inventive we can be in encouraging love and helping out, not avoiding worshiping together as some do but spurring each other on, especially as we see the big Day approaching" (Heb. 10:24–25 MSG).

Worship demonstrably. Let your body express what your heart is feeling. And let your heart be awakened by your body. "May the lifting up of my hands be like the evening sacrifice" (Ps. 141:2). "Because your love is better than life, my lips will glorify you. I will praise you as long as I live, and in your name I will lift up my hands" (Ps. 63:3–4).

Yes, outward expressions of worship can be used inappropriately. People show off. They strut. They worship to be seen. But don't let potential abuse preclude appropriate use. Lift your hands. Clap your hands. Bend your knees. Bow your head. Fall down on your face.

Something powerful happens when we worship.

Something powerful happened the day that the soldiers did. It was Christmas Eve 1915 near the village of Laventie in northern France. World War I was raging. Bombs shook the soil of Europe. Frigid temperatures shook the bones of the fighters. Germans were entrenched on one side and the Royal Welsh Fusiliers on the other. Most of the soldiers were only a few years removed from boyhood. They were young, homesick, and longing to be with loved ones. The guns had blazed in relentless fury for months. Christmas seemed far away from this blood-soaked land.

At one point from the German side of the field came a chorus of voices singing a Welsh holiday hymn in German.

> Sleep my child and peace attend thee,
> All through the night
> Guardian angels God will send thee,
> All through the night
> Soft the drowsy hours are creeping
> Hill and vale in slumber sleeping,
> I my loving vigil keeping
> All through the night.[5]

Soldiers on both sides set down their weapons. For a moment, in that moment, there was no war; there were no enemies; there was just the song. What happened next could only be described as a miracle. The night was spent in carol singing. Around dawn the feelings of goodwill emboldened the soldiers to step out of their trenches and greet their foes. Shouting such greetings as "Hello, Tommy" and "Hello,

Fritz," they shook hands in no-man's-land and exchanged gifts. German beer, sausages, and spiked helmets from one side. Canned corned beef, biscuits, and tunic buttons from the other.

Then, of all things, a game broke out. A form of soccer. It was disjointed and unorganized with perhaps as many as fifty players on each side. For half an hour or so, the battlefield became a soccer field, and enemies enjoyed time together.[6]

And it all began with worship.

We can only pray that an armistice would happen again. That warriors would become worshippers. That we would lay down our weapons of pride and vengeance and join hearts to thank the One who came to bring peace on earth and goodwill to all.

Someday that peace will come. Conflict will give way to an eternal chorus. Until then, we can practice.

> Give Jesus the gift the angels
> gave him, the gift of praise.

Give Jesus the gift the angels gave him, the gift of praise. Don the robe of grace, soar on wings of faith, and take your place in the heavenly chorus and sing, "Glory to God in the highest."

7

God Guides the Wise

*H*oliday time is highway time. Ever since the magi packed their bags for Bethlehem, the birth of Jesus has caused people to hit the road. Our Christmas trips have a lot in common with the one of the wise men. We don't camp with camels, but we have been known to bump into a knobby-kneed in-law on the way to the bathroom. We don't keep an eye out for star lights, but flashing lights of the highway patrol? We watch for them at every curve. And we don't ride in a spice-road caravan, but six hours in a minivan with four kids might have made the wise men thankful for animals.

It's not always ho ho ho on the high, high highway. Extended time in the car reveals human frailties.

Dads refuse to stop. They hearken back to the examples of their forefathers. Did the pioneers spend the night at a Holiday Inn? Did Lewis and Clark ask for directions? Did Joseph allow Mary to stroll through a souvenir shop on the road to Bethlehem? By no means. Men drive as if they have a biblical mandate to travel far and fast, stopping only for gasoline.

And children? Road trips do to kids what a full moon does to the wolf man. If one child says, "I like that song," you might expect the other to say, "That's nice." Won't happen. Instead the other child will reply, "It stinks and so do your feet."

There is also the issue of JBA—juvenile bladder activity. A child can go weeks without going to the bathroom at home. But once on the road, the kid starts leaking like secrets in Washington. On one drive to Colorado, my daughters visited every toilet in New Mexico.

The best advice for traveling with young children is to be thankful they aren't teenagers. Teens are embarrassed by what their parents say, think, wear, eat, and sing. So for their sakes (and if you ever want to see your future grandchildren), don't smile at the waitstaff, don't breathe, and don't sing with the window down or up.

It's wiser to postpone traveling with children until they are a more reasonable age—like forty-two.

Christmas and travel. The first has a way of prompting the second and has done so ever since the delegation from the distant land came searching for Jesus.

Jesus was born in Bethlehem in Judea, during the reign of King Herod. About that time some wise men from eastern lands arrived in Jerusalem, asking,

"Where is the newborn king of the Jews?" (Matt. 2:1–2 NLT)

Matthew loved the magi. He gave their story more square inches of text than he gave the narrative of the birth of Jesus. He never mentions the shepherds or the manger, but he didn't want us to miss the star and the seekers. It's easy to see why. Their story is our story. We're all travelers, all sojourners. In order to find Jesus, every one of us needs direction. God gives it. The story of the wise men shows us how.

In order to find Jesus, every one of us needs direction. God gives it.

We have seen His star in the East and have come to worship Him. (v. 2 NKJV)

God uses the natural world to get our attention. Earth and stars form the first missionary society. "The heavens declare the glory of God" (Ps. 19:1 NKJV). As Paul wrote, "The basic reality of God is plain enough. Open your eyes and there it is! By taking a long and thoughtful look at what God has created, people have always been able to see what their eyes as such can't see: eternal power, for instance, and the mystery of his divine being" (Rom. 1:19–20 MSG).

God led the wise men to Jerusalem with a star. But to lead them to Jesus, he used something else:

> King Herod was deeply disturbed when he heard this, as was everyone in Jerusalem. He called a meeting of the leading priests and teachers of religious law and asked, "Where is the Messiah supposed to be born?"
>
> "In Bethlehem in Judea," they said, "for this is what the prophet wrote:
>
> > 'And you, O Bethlehem in the land of Judah,
> >
> > > are not least among the ruling cities of Judah,
> >
> > for a ruler will come from you
> >
> > > who will be the shepherd for my people Israel.'"
> >
> > (Matt. 2:3–6 NLT)

The star sign was enough to lead the magi to Jerusalem. But it took Scripture to lead them to Jesus.

People see signs of God every day. Sunsets that steal the breath. Newborns that bring tears. Migrating geese that stir a smile. But do all who see the signs draw near to God? No. Many are content simply to see the signs. They do not realize that the riches of God are intended to turn us toward him. "Perhaps you do not understand that God is kind to you so you will change your hearts and lives" (Rom. 2:4 NCV).

The wise men, however, understood the purpose of the sign.

They followed it to Jerusalem, where they heard about the scripture. The prophecy told them where to find Christ. It is interesting to note that the star reappeared *after* they learned about the prophecy. The star "came and stood shining *right over* the place where the Child was" (Matt. 2:9, emphasis mine).[1] It is as if the sign and word worked together to bring the wise men to Jesus. The ultimate aim of all God's messages, both miraculous and written, is to shed the light of heaven on Jesus.

The ultimate aim of all God's messages, both miraculous and written, is to shed the light of heaven on Jesus.

They came to the house where the child was and saw him with his mother, Mary, and they bowed down and worshiped him. They opened their gifts and gave him treasures of gold, frankincense, and myrrh. (v. 11 NCV)

Behold the first Christian worshippers. The simple dwelling became a cathedral. Seekers of Christ found him and knelt in his presence. They gave him gifts: gold for a king, frankincense for a priest, and myrrh for his burial.

They found the Christ because they heeded the sign and believed the scripture.

Noticeably absent at the manger were the scholars of the Torah. They reported to Herod that the Messiah would be born in Bethlehem. Did they not read the prophecy? Yes, but they did not respond to it. You'd think at a minimum they would have accompanied the magi to Bethlehem. The village was near enough. The risk was small enough. At worst they would be out the effort. At best they would see the fulfillment of prophecy. But the priests showed no interest.

The wise men earned their moniker because they did. Their hearts were open to God's gift. The men were never the same again. After worshiping the Christ child, "they departed for their own country another way" (v. 12 NKJV). Matthew uses the word *way* in other places to suggest a direction of life. He speaks of the narrow way (7:13–14 NASB) and "the way of righteousness" (21:32). He may be telling us that the wise men went home as different men.

Called by a sign. Instructed by Scripture. And directed home by God.

It's as if all the forces of heaven cooperated to guide the wise men.

God uses every possible means to communicate with you. The wonders of nature call to you. The promises and prophecies of Scripture speak to you. God himself reaches out to you. He wants to help you find your way home.

Many years ago I watched the television adaptation of

the drama *The Miracle Worker*, the compelling story of two females with great resolve: Helen Keller and Anne Sullivan. Helen was born in 1880. She wasn't yet two when she contracted an illness that left her blind, deaf, and mute. When Helen was seven years old, Annie, a young, partially blind teacher, came to the Kellers' Alabama home to serve as Helen's teacher.

Helen's brother James tried to convince Annie to quit. The teacher wouldn't consider it. She was resolved to help Helen function in a world of sight and sound. Helen was as stubborn as her teacher. Locked in a frightening, lonely world, she misinterpreted Annie's attempts. The result was a battle of wills. Over and over Annie pressed sign language into Helen's palm. Helen pulled back. Annie persisted. Helen resisted.

Finally, in a moment of high drama, a breakthrough. During a fevered exchange near the water pump, Annie placed one of Helen's hands under the spout of flowing water. Into the other hand she spelled out w-a-t-e-r. Over and over, w-a-t-e-r. Helen pulled back. Annie kept signing. W-a-t-e-r.

All of a sudden Helen stopped. She placed her hand on her teacher's and repeated the letters w-a-t-e-r. Annie beamed. She lifted Helen's hand onto her own cheek and nodded vigorously. "Yes, yes, yes! W-a-t-e-r." Helen spelled it again: w-a-t-e-r. Helen pulled Annie around the yard, spelling out the words. G-r-o-u-n-d. P-o-r-c-h. P-u-m-p. It was a victory parade.[2]

Christmas celebrates a similar moment for us—God breaking through to our world. In a feeding stall of all places. He will not leave us in the dark. He is the pursuer, the teacher. He won't sit back while we miss out. So he entered our world. He sends signals and messages: H-o-p-e. L-i-f-e. He cracks the shell of our world and invites us to peek into his. And every so often a seeking soul looks up.

God will not leave us in the dark. He is the pursuer, the teacher. He won't sit back while we miss out. So he entered our world.

May you be one of them.

When God sends signs, be faithful. Let them lead you to Scripture.

As Scripture directs, be humble. Let it lead you to worship.

And as you worship the Son, be grateful. He will lead you home. Who knows? Perhaps before Jesus comes again, we'll discover why men don't ask for directions. Then we can pursue the other great question of life: Why do women apply makeup while they are driving?

But that's a question for ones wiser than I.

8

Humility Shines

*M*ost of the players in the Christmas drama inspire us with their faith.

Mary, who had great courage.

Joseph, who was obedient.

The shepherds, who came quickly and worshipped willingly.

The wise men, who traveled far and gave generously.

Most of the characters in the Bethlehem drama behaved like heroes. But there was one who played the role of a villain.

Then Herod, when he had secretly called the wise men, determined from them what time the star appeared. And he sent them to Bethlehem and said, "Go and search carefully for the young Child, and when you have found Him, bring back word to me, that I may come and worship Him also." . . .

Then Herod, when he saw that he was deceived by the wise men, was exceedingly angry; and he sent forth and put to death all the male children who were in Bethlehem and in all its districts, from two years old and under, according to the time which he had determined from the wise men. Then was fulfilled what was spoken by Jeremiah the prophet, saying:

"A voice was heard in Ramah,

Lamentation, weeping, and great mourning,

Rachel weeping for her children,

Refusing to be comforted,

Because they are no more." (Matt. 2:7–8, 16–18 NKJV)

Herod and the magi share the same chapter, but they didn't share the same heart. The wise men traveled a great distance to see Jesus. Herod refused to leave his own city. The wise men presented their treasures to honor the child. Herod attempted to kill him. The wise men saw Jesus. But Herod? He saw no one but himself. As a result, his obituary forever contains the sad designation: the first person to reject Jesus Christ.

Dean Farrar, a nineteenth-century British scholar, gave this sobering assessment of the king: "His whole career was red with the blood of murder. . . . Deaths by strangulation, deaths by burning, deaths by being cleft asunder, deaths by secret assassination, confessions forced by unutterable torture, acts of insolent and inhuman lust . . . the survivors during his lifetime were even more miserable than the sufferers."[1]

Herod killed three of his own sons. Caesar Augustus once declared, "It is better to be Herod's hog than his son."[2] What happened to the king? What caused him to commit such violent acts?

Pride. Herod was hooked on his own importance. His arrogance blinded his view of Christ. His ego was threatened the moment he heard the magi's question: "Where is He who has been born King of the Jews?" (Matt. 2:2 NKJV).

Herod was "deeply disturbed by their question" (v. 3 TLB). *King of the Jews? Why, that is my title! That is my assignment!* Under the pretense of interest, Herod asked the temple priests and scholars where the Messiah would be born. When Herod learned the answer, he told the wise men, "Go and search carefully for the young Child, and when you have found Him, bring back word to me, that I may come and worship Him also" (v. 8 NKJV).

He could not bring himself to say, "Search for the king." He could only muster, "Search for the child." He didn't have the integrity to make the three-hour trip or even to send an agent from his court but instead relied on the stargazers to find the child. The wise men did so, yet having been warned in a dream to go home another way, they bypassed Herod on their return trip. Their detour left the megalomaniac livid and bloodthirsty, which resulted in the Bethlehem holocaust.

Just as the same shaft of sunlight in a barn can cause birds to sing and rats to scurry, the same message stirred the worship of the wise men and activated the ire of the king. Herod knew enough to realize that the star and scripture were a forecast of the Messiah, but he used that knowledge to carry out an infanticide. Believing is not obedience, and pride eclipses the right choice from us, even when we know the truth. They say love is blind, but pride is blinder.

Herod's pride hurt other people.

Doesn't it always?

How many apologies has self-importance silenced? How many compliments has arrogance muted? How many broken hearts trace their wounds to someone's stubborn, unyielding, my-way-or-the-highway attitude?

Haughtiness hurts people.

The other day I saw some children at play on a large vacant lot where someone had dumped a mound of dirt. They were playing the greatest of kid games: King of the Mountain. The rules are as simple as they are brutal: fight your way to the top, and shove off anyone who threatens to take your spot. It was a slugfest of crawling, pushing, and falling.

King of the Mountain is not just a kid's game. Versions are played in every dormitory, classroom, boardroom, and bedroom. And since mountaintop real estate is limited, people get shoved around. Mark it down: if you want to be king, someone is going to suffer. Your uppitiness won't prompt a Bethlehem massacre, but it might prompt a broken marriage, an estranged friendship, or a divided office.

Pride comes at a high price.

Don't pay it. Consider the counsel of the apostle Paul: "Do not think of yourself more highly than you ought" (Rom. 12:3).

"How much larger your life would be if your self could become smaller in it," wrote G. K. Chesterton. "You would break out of this tiny and tawdry theatre in which your own little plot is always being played, and you would find yourself under a freer sky."[3]

Some time ago I was honored with a nice recognition. A friend learned about it and said, "Max, God gave you that honor because you were humble enough not to let it go to your head." What kind words! The more I thought about what he had said, the better it felt. The more I thought, the more I agreed. As the day went on, I felt better and better about being so humble. I was proud of my humility. That evening I was just about to tell Denalyn what he had said when I felt a conviction. I was about to brag about being humble!

Humility. The moment you think you have it, you don't. Pursue it anyway.

A recurring message of Scripture is that God loves the humble heart. Jesus said, "I am gentle and humble in heart" (Matt. 11:29 NASB). "Though the LORD is supreme, he takes care of those who are humble" (Ps. 138:6 NCV). God says, "I . . . live with people who are humble" (Isa. 57:15 GNT). He also says, "These are the ones I look on with favor: those who are humble and contrite" (Isa. 66:2).

And to the humble, God gifts great treasures.

He gives honor: "Humility goes before honor" (Prov. 15:33 NRSV).

To the humble, God gifts great treasures.

He gives wisdom: "With the humble is wisdom" (Prov. 11:2 NKJV).

He gives direction: "He . . . teaches the humble his way" (Ps. 25:9 NRSV).

And most significantly, he gives grace: "God . . . gives grace to the humble" (1 Peter 5:5 NKJV).

And this reassurance: "He crowns the humble with salvation" (Ps. 149:4 WEB).

God loves humility. And by the same token he hates arrogance. He doesn't dislike arrogance. He doesn't disapprove of arrogance. He hates arrogance.

"I hate pride and arrogance" (Prov. 8:13).

"Everyone proud in heart is an abomination to the LORD" (Prov. 16:5 NKJV).

God says, "Do nothing out of . . . vain conceit" (Phil. 2:3) and "Do not let arrogance come out of your mouth" (1 Sam. 2:3 NASB). Just as he gives grace to the humble, "God opposes the proud" (1 Peter 5:5). Just as humility goes before honor, "a proud attitude leads to ruin" (Prov. 16:18 NCV).

Ponder your achievements less; ponder Christ's more. Spend less time on your throne and more at his cross. Brag on his work, not yours. You are valuable, but you aren't invaluable. It is Christ who matters, not us.

Learn a lesson from the sad life of Herod. It's always better to step down from the pedestal than to be pulled off of it. Like the innkeeper, Herod missed an opportunity to see Jesus. God did everything necessary to get Herod's attention. He sent messengers from the East and a message from the Torah. He sent wonders from the sky and words from Scripture. He sent the testimony of the heavens and the teaching of the prophets. But Herod refused to listen. He chose his puny dynasty over Christ.

He died a miserable old man.

—⊗⊗⊗—

Ponder your achievements less;
ponder Christ's more.
Brag on his work, not yours.

—⊗⊗⊗—

"Realizing how the people disliked him, he ordered his sister Salome and her husband Alexas to slay all the leaders in the hippodrome at the moment of his death, in order to ensure national mourning rather than a festival."[4] The massacre did not occur. His final decree, like his life, proved empty and vain.

Make the wiser choice. The path marked Pride will lead you over a cliff. The path marked Humility will take you to the manger of the Messiah.

9

Perhaps Today

'Tis the season to be looking.
Looking for
  snow if it's cold,
    mistletoe if he's dense,
      instructions if some assembly is required.
Looking for
  red-nose lights if you're young,
    headlights if you're a grandma,
      insights if you're a preacher.
      'Tis the season to be looking.
The first Christmas was marked by "lookers" as well. Joseph looked for lodging. Mary looked into the prunish face of Jesus. A thousand angels looked upon the King. The wise men looked at the star. But no one was looking with more intensity than a seasoned saint named Simeon.

Now there was a man in Jerusalem called Simeon, who was righteous and devout. He was waiting for the consolation of Israel, and the Holy Spirit was on him. It had been revealed to him by the Holy Spirit that he would not die before he had seen the Lord's Messiah. Moved by the Spirit, he went into the temple courts. When the parents brought in the child Jesus to do for him what the custom of the Law required, Simeon took him in his arms and praised God, saying:

> "Sovereign Lord, as you have promised,
> > you may now dismiss your servant in peace.
> For my eyes have seen your salvation,
> > which you have prepared in the sight of all nations:
> a light for revelation to the Gentiles,
> > and the glory of your people Israel." (Luke 2:25–32)

Unlike Joseph and Mary, Simeon did not witness Jesus' birth. Unlike the wise men, he did not visit the child in Bethlehem. By the time he saw Jesus, the feeding stall was occupied only by animals, the manger held only hay. Mary and Joseph had caught up on their sleep. The shepherds were back with their sheep.

Forty days had passed. We can know the time with certainty because of the Jewish law. According to the Torah the mother became ceremonially unclean upon the birth of her child.[1] On the eighth day a male baby was circumcised. After an additional thirty-three days, the parents offered a sacrifice (Lev. 12:1–8).

A baby dedication of sorts.

It was at this dedication that Simeon saw Jesus.

Simeon was likely an old man—gray haired, white bearded. The years had etched his skin and slowed his step and bent his back. He was waiting for the day when "God would take away Israel's sorrow" (Luke 2:25 NCV). A day in which God would end the alienation of the people and reconcile them to himself.

Simeon knew this day would come in his day. "The Holy Spirit had revealed to him that he would not die until he had seen him—God's anointed King" (v. 26 TLB).

How did the Spirit tell Simeon? In a dream? A vision? A scripture? We don't know. But we do know that Simeon lived with an eye toward the future.

Many years ago I preached a sermon about the return of Christ. I had two words, *Perhaps Today*, printed on a piece of paper and given to the members of the congregation. Recently I was in the home of a member and noticed the sheet, framed and placed in a prominent position.

Simeon would have wanted a copy for his wall. He lived with a "perhaps today" attitude. He knew he would see the Messiah on earth before he saw the Father in heaven. And on the fortieth day after Jesus' birth, the day arrived. "The Spirit led Simeon to the Temple" (v. 27 NCV).

Perhaps he had other plans. Maybe he was going to stay home or visit the grandkids. Perhaps his garden needed watering or the dog needed walking. But then came a nudging, a knowing, a prompting. He decided, *I think I'll go to the temple.*

Simeon wound his way through the narrow streets and over the cobblestone paths. Finally he entered the temple courts. Though Simeon had ascended the temple steps a hundred times, the sight of Herod's masterpiece must have moved him. The massive stones. The gilded roof and great colonnades.[2] Even when it wasn't a holiday, the streets were full of worshippers and pilgrims. Somehow, in spite of the multitude, Simeon spotted Joseph and Mary.

No one else had reason to notice the young parents. Angels did not cast petals or blast trumpets at their arrival. Jesus did not ride on a pillow or in a chariot. He had no halo or glow or aura. He gurgled. He nursed. He slept.

Besides, any passerby had a more important quest. People journeyed to the temple for one reason: to encounter God. No one imagined looking for him in the arms of a simple girl from Nazareth.

No one, that is, except Simeon. "Perhaps today," he whispered to himself as he saw them. He walked briskly across the temple courtyard. He excused his way through the pilgrims and caught up with Joseph. "Pardon me," he said. The Nazarene couple stopped and turned.

Mary's belly was no longer round, but her face was. She had the simple softness of a peasant girl. Joseph wore the scratchy robe of a worker. A year earlier he might have objected to the interruption. But the last few months had been marked by surprises. Angels had spoken and worshipped; shepherds had come and gone. His wife knew childbirth before she knew his bed. Joseph was learning to expect the unexpected. So he tilted his head and waited for Simeon to speak.

And Simeon did. "May I?" He gestured to the child.

The same Spirit that had nudged the older man prompted the younger one, and Joseph nodded. Mary gave Jesus to Simeon, and he "took the baby in his arms and thanked God: 'Now, Lord, you can let me, your servant, die in peace as you said. With my own eyes I have seen your salvation, which you prepared before all people'" (vv. 28–31 NCV).

Simeon's response has come to be known in Latin as *Nunc Dimittis*, or "Now Dismiss."[3] *Now* is a timeline term. It indicates the arrival of a moment. "Now we can go." "Now we can eat." "Now we can start." Simeon saw the arrival of Jesus as a "now" moment, the first day of a new era. Now everything was different. The "consolation of Israel" had begun. The gate of history had swung on the hinge of a Bethlehem gate. The Author of life had turned the page and was ready to write a new chapter.

Simeon did not know the name of the chapter, but we do. Scripture denotes this period as "the last days." Paul said, "In the last days there will be many troubles" (2 Tim. 3:1 NCV). Peter urged us to understand "what will happen in the last days" (2 Peter 3:3 NCV). The author of Hebrews wrote, "But now in these last days God has spoken to us through his Son" (1:2 NCV).

We live between the Advents.

The Second Advent will include the sudden, personal, visible, bodily return of Christ. Jesus promised, "I will come again" (John 14:3 RSV). The author of Hebrews declared, "Christ . . . will appear a second time, not to deal with sin but to save those who are eagerly waiting for him" (9:28 RSV).

As he came, Christ will come. But he won't come *as* he came.

He came quietly in Bethlehem. He will return in glory with a shout. "All who are in their graves will hear his voice and come out" (John 5:28–29).

In Bethlehem, Joseph placed Jesus
in a manger. At his return Jesus
will be seated on a throne.

In Bethlehem the just-born Jesus slept. When he returns, "the Lord himself will come down from heaven, with a loud command, with the voice of the archangel and with the trumpet call of God" (1 Thess. 4:16).

At his first coming few noticed. At his second "all the nations of the world will be gathered before him" (Matt. 25:32 NCV).

In Bethlehem, Joseph placed Jesus in a manger. At his return Jesus will be seated on a throne: "The Son of Man will come again in his great glory, with all his angels. He will be King and sit on his great throne" (Matt. 25:31 NCV).

"*What will happen next,* and what we hope for, is what God promised: a new heaven and a new earth where justice reigns" (2 Peter 3:13 *The Voice*). History is not an endless succession of meaningless circles but a directed movement toward a great event. God has a timeline. And because of Bethlehem, we have an idea where we stand on it. As the apostle John said, "My dear children, these are the last days" (1 John 2:18 NCV). We enjoy the fruit of the first coming but anticipate the glory of the second. We refuse to believe that this present world is the sum total of human existence. We celebrate the First Advent to whet our appetites for the Second. We long for the next coming.

God has a timeline. And because
of Bethlehem, we have an idea
where we stand on it.

I found a metaphor for this longing in the West Texas oil fields. My father thought Christmas break was an opportunity for his son to make some good cash. Anyone who could dig a ditch and endure the cold wind would make money.

So as a teenager I spent many a December day in the vast flatlands of the Permian Basin.

The routine was simple. A foreman would drive a truck full of workers to the edge of civilization and show us the ditch that had been dug with a large machine. The furrow was about six feet deep. Before pipe could be placed inside it, the excess rocks and dirt needed to be removed. He would say, "Get to work. I'll come back for you." And then he would drive off.

A root canal would have been more pleasant. Nothing blocks the cold prairie wind in December. It chills the bone. We were miles from another human being. A person can see forever out there. If only there were something to see! We had nothing to do but dig, so we did. All day. By midafternoon we began thinking, *Maybe the foreman's on his way.*

By four o'clock our backs would be tired. We'd lift our heads from the ditch and sweep the horizon. "Does anyone see him?"

By five o'clock we were digging, then looking, digging, then looking.

By sunset, when the already-cold air would turn icy, we would begin to encourage one another with words like "He'll be here soon." We'd think about the dinner that awaited us. The warm house, the hot bath. And just when we thought we couldn't wait any longer, a set of familiar headlights would come bouncing over the horizon. No one had to tell us to climb out of the ditch and gather our tools.

We were ready when he came to take us home.

Some of you have been digging a long time. You're tired from the toil. The ditch is deep, and the work seems endless. You carry the burden of a broken heart. You've walked a long, lonely road. The wind is a cold one, and the world seems as barren as a prairie. You have searched the horizon for the coming of the King. You're wondering, *Is he really coming for us?*

Your wait is nearly over. If all of history were but a year, the leaves would now be autumn gold.

If all of history were merely a day, the sun would have begun to set.

If all of history were just an hour, the minute hands of the clock would be nearing full circle.

Some people say they know the day and the hour of his return. I don't. But I do know the Bible urges us to look for specific signs that point to the return of Christ.

- The preaching of the gospel to all nations (Matt. 24:14; Mark 13:10)
- Days of distress in which saints will suffer and the creation will tremble (Mark 13:7–8, 19–20)
- The coming of the Antichrist, an enemy of God who will deceive many (2 Thess. 2:1–10)
- Salvation of many Jews (Rom. 11:12, 25–26)
- Signs in the heavens (Mark 13:24–25)
- False prophets (Mark 13:22)

To a certain degree each of these signs has seen fulfillment. The gospel has gone around the world. Many
Christians experience severe oppression. The world has
suffered at the hands of global villains. Many Jews have
been saved. Our earth has shaken from birth pangs, and the
church has been weakened by false prophets.

Certainly, these signs will see further fulfillment. But
this much is sure: the end is near. Or, better said, the *beginning* is near.

> Lo, the days are hastening on
> By prophets seen of old.
> When with the ever circling years
> Shall come the time foretold.
> When peace shall over all the earth
> Its ancient splendors fling.
> And the whole world give back the song
> Which now the angels sing.[4]

'Tis the season to be looking not for a jolly man in a red
suit but for a grand King on a white horse. At his command
the sea will give up the dead, the Devil will give up his quest,
kings and queens will give up their crowns, broken hearts
will give up their despair, and God's children will lift up
their worship. Wise is the saint who searches like Simeon.
If you knew Jesus was returning tomorrow, how would you

feel today? Anxious, afraid, unprepared? If so, you can take care of your fears by placing your trust in Christ. If your answer includes words like *happy*, *relieved*, and *excited*, hold tightly to your joy. Heaven is God's answer to any suffering you may face.

If you knew Jesus was coming tomorrow, what would you do today? Then do it! Live in such a way that you would not have to change your plans.

In an earlier chapter I mentioned the sorrow that plagued our family one December. Our daughter suffered a miscarriage during the Advent season. The next year, however, the sorrow was replaced with joy. Christmas brought the excitement of her healthy pregnancy. So healthy, in fact, that Jenna gave each of us an assignment. She was at the point in her pregnancy when the baby was developing the ability to hear. So she asked family members to record audio messages that she could play for her yet-to-be-born daughter.

Who could refuse such an opportunity? I retreated to a quiet corner and captured this welcome.

Dear, dear child. We are so excited to welcome you into the world. We are waiting for you. Your parents have prepared a place for you. You have grandparents, aunts, and uncles ready to shower you with love. We cannot wait to spend time loving you and showing you your wonderful new home.

109

Only after I finished did I realize that is God's invitation to us! He has prepared a place. He has a family to love us. And he has a sparkling new world to show us. Who knows? This could be the day of our delivery.

10

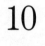

Crown, Cradle, and Cross

The large box sat unexplained in the corner of our living room for weeks. It appeared soon after Thanksgiving and sat untouched throughout most of December. It was as tall as I was, which isn't saying much. I was only four years old. Unlike the other boxes near the Christmas tree, this one bore no glistening wrapping paper or shiny ribbons. It displayed no name, neither of giver nor receiver. It was taped shut, tightly shut, or my brother and I would have opened it. All we could do was ask about it.

Mom had no explanation. She seemed unimpressed. "Just something your dad bought for Christmas." If anything, she assumed Dad had used Christmas as an excuse to buy himself a gift. He'd always wanted an outboard motor to mount on a fishing boat. Did the box contain one?

On Christmas morning while my older sisters opened gifts and my brother and I scampered about playing with our new toys, my mom noticed the still-unopened gorilla of a box.

"Jack," she said, "aren't you going to open the big present?"

Dad could no more keep a straight face than he could walk to the moon on a moonbeam. He began to smile, his eyebrows arched like little rainbows, and he looked at her with a Santa sort of twinkle. "That gift isn't for me; it's for you."

My brother and I stopped and looked. Dad winked at us. We looked at Mom. She was looking at Dad. We knew something fun was about to happen. Mom stepped toward the box. Dad grabbed the 8-millimeter camera, and we kids scurried over.

Mom pried open the top of the nondescript, unaddressed box. She reached in and pulled out nothing but tissue paper. One armful after another.

A remarkable gift can arrive
in an unremarkable package.
One did in Bethlehem.

The image in the film, which our family later loved to watch, rewind, and watch again, begins to shake as Dad begins to giggle. "Keep digging, Thelma," he says from behind the camera.

"What's in here?" she asks, still pulling out paper. Finally she strikes pay dirt. A box within the box. She opens it to find another box. She opens it, then another. This happens a couple more times until at last she reaches the smallest of the boxes. A ring box. My brother and I shout, "Open it, Mom!" She smiles at the camera. "Jack."

I didn't understand the romantic significance of a new ring. But I did learn a lesson: a remarkable gift can arrive in an unremarkable package. One did in the Lucado house.

One did in Bethlehem.

No one expected God to come the way he did. Yet the way he came was every bit as important as the coming itself. The manger is the message. At least this was the opinion of the apostle Paul.

Paul. His name seldom appears in Christmas reflections. We typically think of Joseph, Mary, the shepherds, and the magi. We don't often refer to the reformed Pharisee. Yet we should. His words are the Bible's most eloquent summary of the Bethlehem promise. The descended Christ is now the ascended Christ, and he reigns over us.

In your relationships with one another, have the same mindset as Christ Jesus:

Who, being in very nature God,
did not consider equality with God something
to be used to his own advantage;
rather, he made himself nothing

by taking the very nature of a servant,

being made in human likeness.

And being found in appearance as a man,

he humbled himself

by becoming obedient to death—even death on

a cross!

Therefore God exalted him to the highest place

and gave him the name that is above every name,

that at the name of Jesus every knee should bow,

in heaven and on earth and under the earth,

and every tongue acknowledge that Jesus Christ

is Lord,

to the glory of God the Father. (Phil. 2:5–11)

The apostle was not writing a Christmas sermon. His aim was far more mundane. Paul was counseling a church. The Christians in Philippi seemed to have a few issues, selfish ambition and conceit being among them (2:3). Later in his letter he mentions two women, Euodia and Syntyche. They couldn't get along. Paul was urging them to "be of the same mind in the Lord" (4:2). Paul was appealing to the church to seek humility. As a result we have this four-chapter letter. In the heart of the epistle is the heart of the gospel. A six-verse summary of God's divine intervention. Some scholars think the text is a hymn. If so, then the words compose one of the earliest Christian hymns. Others describe the pericope as a liturgy that was read in the first churches. Still others believe the passage was originally a poem. I like that thought: Paul the poet laureate of Advent. Whether it is a hymn, a liturgy, or a poem from the pen of the apostle, we know this: the reading is eloquent.

Jesus was "in very nature God." Before Bethlehem, Jesus had every advantage and benefit of deity. He was boundless, timeless, and limitless. "All things were made through Him, and without Him nothing was made that was made" (John 1:3 NKJV).

Every rock, tree, and planet needs a stamp that says "Made by Jesus." He gets credit for the Whirlpool Galaxy. It contains more than a hundred billion stars.[1] He created our sun. More than a million Earths could fit inside the sun.[2] Jesus fashioned Betelgeuse, which if it were placed at the center of the Earth's solar system would extend out to the orbit of Jupiter.[3] The star Betelgeuse is approximately a thousand times bigger than our sun.[4] Jesus spoke and the bespangled sky happened. He calls each star by name and can fold up the skies as a bedouin would pack his tent.

Paul's headline, however, is not "Christ the Creator"; it is "Christ the Incarnate One." The One who made everything "made himself nothing." Christ made himself small. He made himself dependent upon lungs, a larynx, and legs. He experienced hunger and thirst. He went through all the normal stages of human development. He was taught to walk, stand, wash his face, and dress himself. His muscles grew stronger; his hair grew longer. His voice cracked when he passed through puberty. He was genuinely human.

When he was "full of joy" (Luke 10:21), his joy was authentic. When he wept for Jerusalem (Luke 19:41), his tears were as real as yours or mine. When he asked, "How long must I put up with you?" (Matt. 17:17 NLT), his frustration was honest. When he cried out from the cross, "My God, my God, why have you forsaken me?" (Matt. 27:46), he needed an answer. He knew only what the Father revealed to him (John 12:50). If the Father did not give direction, Jesus did not claim to have it.

He took "the very nature of a servant" (Phil. 2:7). He became like us so he could serve us! He entered the world not to demand our allegiance but to display his affection.

―――∞∞∞―――

> He entered the world not to demand our allegiance but to display his affection.

―――∞∞∞―――

Jesus did not view his equality with God as "something to be grasped" (Phil. 2:6 NET) or "exploited" (NRSV). He refused to throw his weight around. He divested himself of divine advantage.

When people mocked him, he didn't turn them into stones. When soldiers spat on him, he didn't boomerang their spit. When people called him crazy, he didn't strike them blind. Just the opposite. He became "obedient to death—even death on a cross!" (v. 8).

Paul gave special emphasis: "*even* death on a cross" (emphasis mine). Crucifixion was the cruelest form of execution in the Roman Empire. It was commonly reserved for those of the lowest class, especially slaves. It was regulated only by the morality of the executioners, and they had little to speak of. The victim was tortured, whipped, nailed to a beam of wood, and impaled with a spear. He was left naked and bloody, suspended for all to see. He became a public example of how society treats evildoers.

It cannot be said too often that was God on that cross. *God* took the nails. *God* took the whips. *God* bore the shame. *God* felt the tip of the spear. *God* exhaled a final breath.

Jesus descended the ladder of incarnation one rung at a time.

In nature, God.

He did not grasp equality with God.

He made himself nothing.

He took on the form of a servant.

He submitted himself to death.

Even death on a cross.

Down, down, down, down. From heaven's crown to Bethlehem's cradle to Jerusalem's cross.

It was one thing for Christ to enter a womb, quite another for him to be placed in a tomb. But the tomb could not hold him. Paul's poem takes on a triumphant tone. "Therefore God exalted him to the highest place and gave him the name that is above every name" (v. 9).

The One who went low is now made high. The One who descended is now exalted. Jesus is promoted to the "highest place." No angel is higher. No political office is higher. Jesus outranks every ruler and conqueror. Jesus is, right now, in the highest place. He occupies the only true throne in the universe. Every other throne is made of papier-mâché and is doomed to pass. Not the throne of Jesus. God "gave him the name that is above every name" (v. 9).

Names carry clout. When the name *Queen Elizabeth* is announced, people turn. When the letter is signed by John F. Kennedy, it is treasured and stored in a safe-deposit box. Napoleon, Caesar, Alexander the Great—all these names turned heads. But only one name will forever cause them to bow: "At the name of Jesus every knee should bow, in heaven and on earth and under the earth" (v. 10).

The poor. The rich. The black. The brown. The politician. The physician. The red-carpet superstar. The street-corner panhandler. Every knee will bow before Jesus. And "every tongue will confess that Jesus Christ is Lord" (v. 11 NASB).

There are people on our planet who mock the name of Jesus. They scoff at the idea of God on earth. They renounce their need for a Savior and cast aspersions on any who believe in Christ. They are self-sufficient, independent, self-made, and self-reliant. Ask them to bend a knee before

Jesus, and they will laugh at you. But they will not laugh forever. A day is coming in which they will bow in his presence. Stalin will confess his name. Herod will confess his name. Even, or especially, Satan will confess his name. "All who have raged against him will come to him and be put to shame" (Isa. 45:24).

One ruler after another will step forward. Crowns will be collected at the foot of Jesus' throne. So will Pulitzers, Nobels, and gold medals. MVP? PhD? MD? All recognitions will become instantly puny in the presence of Christ the Creator. No one will boast. All the money in history will be shown to be counterfeit. Every Rolls-Royce will seem to be an oxcart. Nothing will matter. No one will matter.

Just Jesus.

On the Great Day you'll hear billions of voices make the identical claim about Jesus Christ. Multitudes of people will bow low like a field of wheat blown by the wind, each one saying to Jesus, "You are the Christ, the Son of the living God" (Matt. 16:16 NKJV).

Those who worshipped him on earth will confess him gladly. Those who didn't will confess him regretfully. Believers will receive their inheritance. Unbelievers will receive theirs: separation from Christ.

In one of his broadcasts C. S. Lewis stated:

God will invade . . . When that happens, it's the end of the world. When the author walks on to the stage the play's over . . . For this time it will be God *without* disguise; something so overwhelming that it will strike either irresistible love or irresistible horror into every creature. It will be too late then to *choose* your side . . . It will be the time when we discover which side we really have chosen.[5]

By the way, Jesus has not surrendered his earthly body. The incarnation that began in Bethlehem continues at this moment in the heavens. When Jesus ascended, he did so in a human body. Having become a man, he will never cease to be a man. The God-in-the-flesh remains exactly that!

Why does this matter? There is a human being in charge of the universe. Glorified, for sure. Exalted, by all means. Utterly divine, certainly. But still, the hand that directs the affairs of humanity is the same hand that held a hammer in Nazareth. In the center of that hand is a scar, an eternal reminder of God's eternal love.

———— ⬿⬿⬿ ————

Humble yourself before the One who humbled himself for you.

———— ⬿⬿⬿ ————

Bow before him. Humble yourself before the One who humbled himself for you.

And to think, it all began in the most inconspicuous of places: a hay box in Bethlehem.

11

It's Good-Bye to the Bents

The Christmas tree hunt is on. Families are entering tents and patrolling sidewalks. They lift limbs and examine needles. They measure. They ponder. They consider. They barter.

The tree can't be too tall or too short. It needs to fit the room and the budget. It must be full yet not dense, mature but not dry. A noble fir for some. A Douglas fir or Virginia pine for others. The preferences are different, but the desire is the same. We want the perfect Christmas tree.

And, oh, the special moment when we find it. When we lash it to the car. Drag it into the house and set it in the tree stand.

We revel in this moment. Only a few people have won the U.S. Open, completed an Ironman triathlon, or qualified as Rhodes Scholars. Fewer still have positioned a Christmas tree so that it doesn't lean.

Throughout the year we prepare. We read articles, attend seminars, swap ideas, and share secrets. We are bonded by the desire to avoid the tragedy of the holiday season: a leaning tree.

One year I barely escaped. Denalyn and I placed the tree in the stand, stood back, and sighed at what we saw. The dreaded tilt. I crawled under the branches and began adjusting the screws until the tree stood as straight as a stalk of wheat. We stepped back and admired my engineering skills. Denalyn placed her arm in mine, and I choked back tears of joy. My children called me blessed. Angels began to sing. The blast of trumpets sounded in the front yard, where neighbors had gathered. The White House called to congratulate me. We strung the lights and hung the decorations. It was a wonderful night.

Then disaster struck. The tree started to lean again. Decorations shook, lights shifted, Denalyn shouted, and I ran to the rescue.

This time I placed the tree on its side, removed the stand, and saw the root of the problem. Just six inches above the cut line was a right turn. Our tree was crooked! Once upon a time in a forest, this tree had been a leaner! And now here it was, in our house, in broad daylight, in front of my own children—leaning again!

What's a person to do? As I was retrieving a saw from the garage, it occurred to me: I'm not the first father to deal with this issue. God faces this situation on a continual basis. Don't we have our share of unattractive bents?

I know I do. Take just the last three days:

- I avoided returning a call to a congregant because most of the time conversations with him generate more whine than Napa Valley. I saw his number on my phone and groaned, "I don't want an earful of his woes." And I'm a pastor! One of his pastors! I'm supposed to love the sheep, feed the sheep, and care for the sheep. And I avoided this sheep. (I eventually called. He wanted to compliment a sermon.)
- I woke up at 2:30 yesterday morning, reliving the outcome of a meeting. I disagreed with a particular decision. When the vote was taken, I was in the minority. And I was ticked off. Between 2:30 a.m. and 3:30 a.m., I convicted each of the other team members of stupidity and insensitivity. My thought pattern was toxic.
- And then there is the issue of a deadline. Will I make it? Why did I agree to it? Why does the publisher demand it? Don't they know it takes space for a fragile soul like mine to create?

Would that I stood as straight as a sequoia, but I don't. And since I don't, I find a kindred spirit in the Christmas tree. I think you will find the same. What you do for a tree, God does for you.

He picked you.

Do you purchase the first tree you see? Of course not. You search for the right one. You walk the rows. You lift several up and set them down. You examine them from all angles until you decide, *This one is perfect*. You have a place in mind where the tree will sit. Not just any tree will do.

God does the same. He knows just the place where you'll be placed. He has a barren living room in desperate need of warmth and joy. A corner of the world needs some color. He selected you with that place in mind.

As King David wrote, "You made my whole being; you formed me in my mother's body. I praise you because you made me in an amazing and wonderful way. What you have done is wonderful. . . . All the days planned for me were written in your book before I was one day old" (Ps. 139:13–14, 16 NCV).

God made you on purpose with a purpose. He interwove calendar and character, circumstance and personality to create the right person for the right corner of the world, and then he paid the price to take you home.

God made you on purpose
with a purpose.

He purchased you.

We don't ask the tree-lot owner to give us the tree for free. The kid who loads the tree in the trunk doesn't shell out the cash; we do. We make the necessary payment.

God did the same. "God bought you with a high price" (1 Cor. 6:20 NLT).

Rick Warren tells about a time he was sitting in a parking lot. His three-year-old daughter was in the backseat in her car seat. As they waited for his wife to come out of the store, his daughter grew restless. Anticipating a short wait, Rick didn't want to remove her. The little girl hung her head out the window and yelled, "Please, God! Get me out of this!"[1]

At some point in life, don't we all feel like Rick's daughter? We are stuck. Not stuck in a backseat, but stuck in a dying body, with bad habits, suffering the consequences of poor choices in a rebellious world. We need help.

So we shop till we drop, drink till we can't think, work till we can't stop. We do anything possible to get our minds off our mess, only to wake up, sober up, or sit up and realize we are still stuck.

So we take pills, take vacations, and take advice from therapists, bartenders, and big brothers. We buy new purses or Porsches. We change hair color, lovers, and the shape of our tummies. But we end up facing the same mess.

We need someone to save us from meaninglessness and meanness. We are lost and need to be found and taken home. We need a Savior. The Christmas promise is this: we have a Savior, and his name is Jesus.

His time on earth was a search-and-rescue mission. He rescued a woman hiding in Samaria. Five husbands had dumped her like the morning garbage. The sixth wouldn't marry her. She was the town scamp. She filled her water bucket in the heat of the day to avoid the stares of the people. Christ went out of his way to help her.[2]

The Christmas promise is this: we have a Savior, and his name is Jesus.

He rescued a demoniac in the caves. Evil spirits had driven the man to mutilate himself, slashing himself with stones. One word from Christ stopped the hurting.[3]

He spotted pint-size Zacchaeus in Jericho. The tax collector had swindled enough people to stockpile his retirement. Yet he would have given it all for a clean conscience and a good friend. One lunch with Jesus and he found both.[4]

Jesus' ministry went on like this for three years. He changed person after person; no one quite knew how to respond to this carpenter who commanded the dead. His healing hands had calluses; his divine voice had an accent. He tended to doze off on boats and grow hungry on trips. Yet he scared the hell out of the possessed and gave hope to the dispossessed. Just when he seemed poised for a crown, he died on a cross.

We don't know why the cross of Christ is often called a tree. Perhaps the earliest crosses were actually trees. Or since crosses were formed from trees, maybe the name stuck. But whatever the reason, the first-century writers often called the cross a tree. Peter did when he declared, "[Jesus] Himself bore our sins in His own body on the tree" (1 Peter 2:24 NKJV).

Somewhere on the timeline between the Tree of Knowledge in the garden and the Tree of Life in heaven is the Tree of Sacrifice near Jerusalem. And if Christmas trees are known for beauty and gifts, then who would deny that the most wonderful Christmas tree was a rugged one on a bald knob? "God . . . loved us and sent His *unique* Son *on a special mission* to become an atoning sacrifice for our sins" (1 John 4:10 *The Voice*). Jesus took on our sin. He was covered by the rebellion that separated us from God. He endured what we should have endured. He paid the price to save us.

> When we were still powerless, Christ died for the ungodly. (Rom. 5:6)

> Christ . . . died for sins once for all, the righteous for the unrighteous, that he might bring us to God. (1 Peter 3:18 RSV)

In the manger God loves you; through the cross God saves you. But has he taken you to his home? Not yet. He has work for you to do. He wants the world to see what God can do with his purchased possessions.

So . . . he prunes you.

He takes an ax to your prejudices and clippers to your self-pity, and when there is a tilt in your character that needs to be removed, he's been known to pull out the old Black & Decker. Jesus said, "My Father is the gardener. . . . He trims and cleans every branch that produces fruit so that it will produce even more fruit" (John 15:1–2 NCV).

———— ∞ ————

In the manger God loves you; through the cross God saves you.

———— ∞ ————

Once he stabilizes us, the decorating begins. He festoons us with the fruit of the Spirit: love, joy, peace, patience, kindness, goodness, faithfulness, gentleness, and self-control (Gal. 5:22–23 NCV). He crowns us. Most people crown their Christmas trees with either an angel or a star. God uses both. He sends his angels to protect us and his Word as a star to guide us.

Then he surrounds us with his grace. We become his depot, the distribution point of God's gifts. He wants no one to leave our presence empty-handed. Some people find the gift of salvation. For others the gifts are smaller: a kind word, a good deed. But all the gifts are from God.

Our task is to stand tall in his love, secure in our place, sparkling in kindness, surrounded by his goodness, freely giving to all who come our way.

⎯⎯∞⎯⎯

You, me, and the Christmas tree. Picked, purchased, and pruned. Trust God's work.

⎯⎯∞⎯⎯

You, me, and the Christmas tree. Picked, purchased, and pruned.

Trust God's work.

You're going to look much better without the bents.

12

—⊸∞⊷—

Every Day a Christmas, Every Heart a Manger

Hollywood would recast the Christmas story. Joseph's collar is way too blue. Mary is green from inexperience. The couple's star power doesn't match the bill. Too obscure. Too simple. The story warrants some headliners. A square-jawed Joseph. Someone of the Clooney vintage. And Mary needs a beauty mark and glistening teeth. Angelina Jolie–ish. And what about the shepherds? Do they sing? If so, perhaps Bono and U2?

Hollywood would recast the story.

A civilized person would sanitize it. No person, however poor, should be born in a cow stall. Hay on the floor. Animals on the hay. Don't place the baby in a feed trough; the donkey's nose has been there. Don't wrap the newborn in rags. They smell like sheep. Speaking of smells, watch where you step.

A good public-relations firm would move the birth to a big city. See what Roman palaces they might rent, what Greek villas they could lease. The Son of God deserves a royal entry. Less peasant, more pizzazz. Out with the heads of sheep, in with the heads of state. Shouldn't we ticker tape this event? You'd think so.

Let stallions prance and trumpets blast. Summon emperors from ancient thrones and palaces not yet built. Abraham and Moses should kneel at the manger. Even Adam and Eve should come to Bethlehem and bow before the Alpha and the Omega, whom Mary holds.

But we didn't design the hour. God did. And God was content to enter the world in the presence of sleepy sheep and a wide-eyed carpenter. No spotlights, just candlelight. No crowns, just cows chewing cud.

God made so little of his Son's coming. He didn't even circle the date on the calendar. Ancient Christmases bounced from date to date before landing on December 25. Some early leaders favored dates in March. For centuries the Eastern Orthodox church celebrated Christmas on January 6, and some still do. Only in the fourth century did the church choose December 25 as the date to celebrate Jesus' coming.[1] We've made bigger deals out of lesser comings. How could this be? No exact date of birth. No hoopla at his birth. Is this a mistake?

Or is this the message?

Maybe your life resembles a Bethlehem stable. Crude in some spots, smelly in others. Not much glamour. Not always neat. People in your circle remind you of stable animals: grazing like sheep, stubborn like donkeys, and that cow in the corner looks a lot like the fellow next door.

You, like Joseph, knocked on the innkeeper's door. But you were too late. Or too old, sick, dull, damaged, poor, or peculiar. You know the sound of a slamming door. So here you are in the grotto, always on the outskirts of activity, it seems.

You do your best to make the best of it, but try as you might, the roof still leaks, and the winter wind still sneaks through the holes you just can't seem to fix. You've shivered through your share of cold nights.

And you wonder if God has a place for a person like you. Find your answer in the Bethlehem stable.

———— ᘒ ————

If you wonder if God has a place
for a person like you, find your
answer in the Bethlehem stable.

———— ᘒ ————

Imagine two angels on a tour of the universe, as J. B. Phillips did. His Christmas analogy casts light on God's love. The angels fly from galaxy to galaxy until they enter the one in which we live. As the sun and its orbiting planets come into view, the senior angel calls attention to a somewhat smaller member of the solar system.

"I want you to watch that one particularly," said the senior angel, pointing with his finger.

"Well, it looks very small and rather dirty to me," said the little angel. "What's special about that one?"

His superior explained that the unimpressive ball was the renowned Visited Planet. The lesser angel was surprised.

"Do you mean that our great and glorious Prince . . . went down in Person to this fifth-rate little ball? . . .

"Do you mean to tell me," he said, "that He stooped so low as to become one of those creeping, crawling creatures of that floating ball?"

"I do, and I don't think He would like you to call them 'creeping, crawling creatures' in that tone of voice. For, strange as it may seem to us, He loves them. He went down to visit them to lift them up to become like Him."[2]

It really comes down to that: God loves us. The story of Christmas is the story of God's relentless love for us.

———∞———

The story of Christmas is the story of God's relentless love for us.

———∞———

Let him love you. If God was willing to wrap himself in rags and drink from a mother's breast, then all questions about his love for you are off the table. You might question his actions, decisions, or declarations. But you can never, ever question his zany, stunning, unquenchable affection.

The moment Mary touched God's face is the moment God made his case: there is no place he will not go. If he is willing to be born in a barnyard, then expect him to be at work anywhere—bars, bedrooms, boardrooms, and brothels. No place is too common. No person is too hardened. No distance is too far. There is no person he cannot reach. There is no limit to his love.

When Christ was born, so was our hope.

———— ✼ ————

When Christ was born, so was our hope.

———— ✼ ————

This is why I love Christmas. The event invites us to believe the wildest of promises: God became one of us so we could become one with him. He did away with every barrier, fence, sin, bent, debt, and grave. Anything that might keep us from him was demolished. He only awaits our word to walk through the door.

Invite him in. Escort him to the seat of honor, and pull out his chair. Clear the table; clear the calendar. Call the kids and neighbors.

Christmas is here. Christ is here.

One request from you, and God will do again what he

did then: scatter the night with everlasting light. He'll be born in you.

Listen as God whispers, "No mess turns me back; no smell turns me off. I live to live in a life like yours. Every heart can be a manger. Every day can be a Christmas. Let 'Silent Night' be sung on summer nights. Let Advent brighten the autumn chill. The Christmas miracle is a year-long celebration."

May this prayer be yours:

My Heart, Your Manger

Like the stable in which you lay,
my heart is simple, frail as hay.
But if you would within me stay,
Make my heart your manger, I pray.
Make my world your Bethlehem,
centerpieced with heaven's Son.
Make this night a shepherd's sky,
quickened bright with holy dawn.
Rush the air with cherub wings.
Brush this earth. Let angels sing.
A glimpse of your face. A taste of your grace.
Be born in this place.
I pray.
Amen

Bethlehem

—⊛—

Advent Devotional Guide

Prepared by Christine Anderson

*E*very year Advent invites us to prepare our hearts once more for the gift—the gift that seemingly is too good to be true but is, in fact, miraculously and joyously true! And each year, we have the opportunity to say yes to that invitation, to prepare our hearts for the miracle of Immanuel, "God with us."

The word *advent* comes from the Latin word *adventus* and simply means "coming" or "arrival." Advent begins each year on the fourth Sunday before Christmas, which is the Sunday closest to November 30. It is a season in which Christians around the world celebrate the First Advent, Jesus' birth, and also anticipate the Second Advent, Christ's return. Although the themes of Advent sometimes vary, those most commonly observed during the four weeks of Advent are hope, peace, joy, and love.

This guide has five devotions—one for each of the four weeks of Advent and one for Christmas Eve/Christmas Day. Each devotion includes the following:

- *Scripture.* Passages traditionally read during Advent are taken from both the Old and New Testaments, and include selections from the Psalms, the Prophets, the Epistles, and the Gospels.
- *Questions for Reflection.* Drawing on the themes of Scripture and related passages from *Because of Bethlehem*, the questions are designed to help you explore the intersection between your life and the Advent theme for each week.
- *Advent Prayer.* You can tuck these brief and simple prayers into your pocket and take them with you wherever you go. Pray them often to bring the promise of each week's theme into every circumstance you encounter.
- *Advent Practice.* Practices provide a way to explore and to respond to what you learn. Each week includes options to help deepen your experience of that week's theme.

As you reflect on the miracle of Christ's birth and the promise of his return, may you experience the true meaning of Christmas: Immanuel, God with us—*God with you.*

Week 1: Hope

⸺⚬⚬⚬⸺

The manger dares us to believe the best is
yet to be. And it could all begin today.

At Advent, we are invited to immerse ourselves
in hope. Biblical hope is not wishful thinking. It
is the unshakable confidence that God can be trusted. It is
the belief that God is always at work for our good (Rom.
8:24–25, 28). It is the assurance that God's promises are
true even while we wait for their fulfillment. Because our
hope is certain, we wait patiently, not fretfully, trusting that
God is already at work to provide the light we seek, the help
we need, and the deliverance we long for.

Scripture

Psalm 80:1–7, 17–19
Isaiah 2:1–5
Romans 13:11–14
Mark 13:24–37

Questions for Reflection

1. Advent is the season to be looking—looking for light, for rescue, for every promised good thing. Each of these Scripture passages reflects some aspect of this eager and hopeful anticipation. The psalmist implored God, "Let your face shine, that we may be saved" (Ps. 80:3 NRSV). The prophet Isaiah charged God's people to "walk in the light of the LORD!" (Isa. 2:5 NRSV). The apostle Paul roused his readers with the command, "Wake from sleep . . . and put on the armor of light" (Rom. 13:11–12 NRSV). And Jesus urged his followers to "keep alert . . . keep awake" (Mark 13:33, 35 NRSV).

   • Which of these four directives from Scripture resonates most with you right now? Why?

   • The emphases on light and alertness indirectly acknowledge other, less-welcome realities, such as darkness, danger, lethargy, and exhaustion. As you anticipate the weeks leading up to Christmas, what unwelcome realities could you be facing?

   • The answer to darkness is light, to danger is rescue, to lethargy is vitality, to exhaustion is rest. Which of

148

these do you think you will need most in the days and
weeks ahead?

2. The prophet Isaiah described an expansive vision
   of what will happen when the hope of the coming
   Messiah is realized: nations "will beat their swords into
   plowshares and their spears into pruning hooks. Nation
   will not take up sword against nation, nor will they
   train for war anymore" (Isa. 2:4). When the Messiah
   reigns, warriors become farm workers, soldiers grow
   vegetables, and troopers till the soil.

   • In what ways does the holiday season (or the stress
     of everyday life) bring out the fight in you—your
     warrior/soldier/trooper instincts? What are your
     weapons of choice, your equivalent of swords and
     spears?

   • If the Messiah is to reign in your life this Advent
     and Christmas, in what situations or relationships
     might you need to lay down your arms? What are
     your equivalents of plowshares and pruning hooks?
     Or how might you exchange your weapons for the
     "armor of light" (Rom. 13:12)?

3. At Advent hope fills us with anticipation—the King is
   coming and we want everything in our lives to be ready
   to receive him! Max puts it this way: "If you knew Jesus
   was coming tomorrow, what would you do today? Then
   do it! Live in such a way that you would not have to
   change your plans" (page 103).

- Allow yourself to imagine that Jesus will make a literal visit to your home and that you have four weeks to get ready. If you want to be at your best and to fully enjoy the visit, how would you prepare?

  I would prepare physically by . . .
  I would prepare relationally by . . .
  I would prepare emotionally by . . .
  I would prepare financially by . . .
  I would prepare spiritually by . . .

- In what ways, if any, would you need to reorder your life or schedule to make this preparation? What would move up on your priority list, and what would move down?

- The culture in Jesus' day placed a very high value on hospitality. Among other things, welcoming an honored guest might include greeting the person with a kiss, pouring oil on the head, and providing water to wash the feet (Luke 7:44–46). Together these gestures created a warm welcome so guests felt not only refreshed and respected but also genuinely wanted and appreciated. What comes to mind when you consider welcoming Jesus in a way that would make him feel not just respected or worshipped but genuinely wanted and appreciated? In what ways, if any, would it change your preparations?

4. Max writes, "The manger . . . dares us to believe the best is yet to be. And it could all begin today" (page 9).

If Advent and Christmas were everything you could hope for this year, what words or phrases would you use to describe them?

Advent Prayer
Come, Lord Jesus. My hope is in you.

Advent Practice
Consider using one or more of the following options to help you practice and experience hope this week.

- Train your heart to seek the light of Christ by noticing all the lights around you throughout the day—everything from sunrise to holiday lights to the little light at the back of the refrigerator. Stuck in rush-hour traffic? Let the brake lights on the car in front of you prompt you to use your Advent Prayer, *Come, Lord Jesus. My hope is in you.* If you find it helpful, keep a daily light list or use your phone to take pictures of all the lights that prompt you to invite the light and hope of Christ into each moment of your day.
- Set aside time for preparation. Briefly review your responses to question 3, and follow through on one or more of the preparations you identified. For example, *I would prepare physically by getting eight hours of sleep each night.* Then work through your schedule for the week(s) ahead, making any necessary changes so you

can prepare for, receive, and truly enjoy the coming of
Christ.

- Make or buy a simple Advent wreath to mark the
progression of Advent from week to week. Light the
appropriate candle(s) each Sunday. You may also choose
to relight them when you pray each day or when you
have your evening meals as a reminder that the light of
Christ is always with you. If this hasn't been a tradition
in your home, now is a good time to begin an annual
Advent tradition with your family.

Advent Hymn

O LITTLE TOWN OF BETHLEHEM

O little town of Bethlehem, how still we see thee lie!
Above thy deep and dreamless sleep the silent stars go by;
Yet in thy dark streets shineth the everlasting Light;
The hopes and fears of all the years are met in thee tonight.

For Christ is born of Mary, and gathered all above,
While mortals sleep, the angels keep their watch of
    wond'ring love.
O morning stars, together proclaim the holy birth!
And praises sing to God, the King, and peace to all
    on earth.

How silently, how silently, the wondrous gift is giv'n!
So God imparts to human hearts the blessings of
    his heav'n.
No ear may hear his coming, but in this world of sin,
Where meek souls will receive him, still the dear Christ
    enters in.

O holy Child of Bethlehem, descend to us, we pray;
Cast out our sin and enter in, be born to us today.
We hear the Christmas angels the great glad tidings tell;
O come to us, abide with us, our Lord Emmanuel!

Lyrics: Phillips Brooks, 1867

⸺⚬⚬⚬⸺

May the God of hope fill you with all joy and peace as you trust in him, so that you may overflow with hope by the power of the Holy Spirit.

Romans 15:13

⸺⚬⚬⚬⸺

Thanks be to God for his indescribable gift!

2 Corinthians 9:15

⸺⚬⚬⚬⸺

Hoping does not mean doing nothing. . . . It is the opposite of desperate and panicky manipulations, of scurrying and worrying. And hoping is not dreaming. It is not spinning an illusion or fantasy to protect us from our boredom or our pain. It means a confident, alert expectation that God will do what he said he will do. It is imagination put in the harness of faith. It is a willingness to let God do it his way and in his time.

Eugene H. Peterson, *A Long Obedience in the Same Direction*

⸺⚬⚬⚬⸺

The Christmas message is that there is hope for a ruined humanity—hope of pardon, hope of peace with God, hope of glory—because at the Father's will Jesus became poor and was born in a stable so that thirty years later he might hang on a cross.

J. I. Packer, *Knowing God*

To prepare our hearts for Christmas, we must cultivate the spirit of expectancy.

Handel H. Brown, *Keeping the Spirit of Christmas*

Hope is patience with the lamp lit.

Tertullian

Week 2: Peace

———— ∞∞∞ ————

Christ came to bring peace on
earth and goodwill to all.

$\mathcal{J}$ust as the ancient Israelites longed for the coming of the Messiah, who would put all things right, Christians long for the return of Christ our King—the one who will come again in glory. Although Christ's return is a day of promise, it is also a day of judgment (Rom. 14:10–12; 2 Tim. 4:1). As we eagerly anticipate the Second Advent, we pause to consider our readiness for Christ's coming and our need to repent of anything that keeps us from being at peace with God.

Scripture

Psalm 85:1–2, 8–13

Isaiah 40:1–11

2 Peter 3:8–15

Matthew 3:1–12

Questions for Reflection

1. The Scripture selections hold in tension several realities about the coming of Christ:

   He will come as both a sovereign Lord *and* a gentle Shepherd (Isa. 40:10–11).

   He will come to destroy *and* to build. He will destroy the heavens and the earth, subjecting everything and everyone to judgment; and he will create a new heaven and earth, where righteousness reigns (2 Peter 3:10, 13).

   He will come to separate *and* to gather. Just as a farmer sorts wheat from chaff at the harvest, Christ will winnow his harvest, burning the chaff with fire and gathering his wheat into the barn (Matt. 3:12).

   His reign will be marked by unfailing love *and* unflinching truth (Ps. 85:10).

   • What is your initial response to these pairings that might be considered opposites? Which of these tensions seems hardest to reconcile?

- Of these descriptions which make the most sense to you?

- In what ways have you recently experienced these dual realities in your relationship with Christ? For example, how has Christ been both your sovereign Lord and your gentle Shepherd? How has an experience of judgment (or conviction) also been an experience of renewal? How has unflinching truth also reassured you of his unfailing love?

- How do these divine principles affect your understanding of ways to prepare yourself during this Advent season for Christ's coming?

2. The psalmist wrote, "I listen carefully to what God the LORD is saying, for he speaks peace to his faithful people." And then he gave this warning: "But let them not return to their foolish ways" (Ps. 85:8 NLT).

- For the psalmist, experiencing peace required listening carefully to what God was saying. Briefly identify the situations or relationships in which you most need peace. What makes it difficult for you to listen carefully to what God might be saying to you in these areas?

- Peace is also intimately connected to righteousness (Ps. 85:10), faithfulness (Ps. 85:11), and a refusal to fall back into foolish ways (Ps. 85:8). How do these anchors for peace help you experience or better understand God's peace in your life?

3. In chapter 3 Max describes an encounter with a pair of teenage boys that got the better of him. In reflecting on the cause of his uncharacteristic behavior, he writes:

> I'd like to blame my behavior on my state of mind, the stress of the traffic, the driver who nearly hit my car, or the passenger who pushed my buttons. But I can blame my bizarre behavior on only one thing. The punk inside me. For a few minutes at a stoplight near a shopping mall, I forgot who I was.
>
> And I forgot who the teenager was. In that heated moment he wasn't someone's son. He wasn't a creation of God. . . . He was a disrespectful jerk, and I let him bring out the disrespectful jerk in me. (page 26)

- Think of a recent experience in which you realized, *That just wasn't me* or *I just wasn't myself.*
- On what did you want to blame your behavior?
- What did you "forget" about yourself and others?

4. "Under the right circumstances you will do the wrong thing," Max writes. "You won't want to. You'll try not to, but you will. Why? You have a sin nature" (page 26).

- What are your "right circumstances," the conditions in which you are prone to do the wrong thing?
- What three words or phrases best describe you when you are under stress or in your "right circumstances"? How do these characteristics differ from the person you believe you really are, or the person you want to be?

- "Jesus not only did a work *for* us," Max writes, "he does a work *within* us" (pages 29–30). In other words, Jesus not only saves us; he wants to change us. Do you tend to focus more on the fact that Jesus saved you, or the fact that he wants to change you? Why?

5. A central task of Advent, and the Christian life as a whole, is to pursue peace with God—to live today with our eternal tomorrow always in mind. The apostle Peter wrote:

> Since everything will be destroyed in this way, what kind of people ought you to be? You ought to live holy and godly lives as you look forward to the day of God and speed its coming. . . . [S]ince you are looking forward to this, make every effort to be found spotless, blameless and at peace with him. (2 Peter 3:11–12, 14)

We are often caught up in the busyness of *doing*. Time is short, and our to-do lists are long, especially during the holidays. But the invitation of this passage is to focus instead on *being*—specifically, being the kind of people we ought to be.

- How might it change your experience of Advent this year if you were to make your priority *being*—the person you want to become—instead of *doing*?
- When you allow yourself to "look forward to the day of God," what thoughts stir in you? What hopes does it kindle for the kind of person you most want to be?

Advent Prayer
Come, Lord Jesus. You are my peace.

Advent Practice
Consider using one or more of the following options to practice and experience peace this week.

- Make a *being* or a *to-be* list, and keep it with your to-do list. Reread 2 Peter 3:11–14. On the pad of paper or electronic device you typically use to create your daily or weekly to-do list, write down a few phrases or statements that describe the person you hope to be. For example, *I want to be a peacemaker in my relationships, I want to be a loving presence*, or *I want to be someone who prioritizes people over projects*. Refer to your to-be list every time you refer to your to-do list—at least once a day—as a way to focus on being at peace with God.
- Set aside a specific time in your calendar this week for self-reflection and confession. In God's loving presence consider the areas where you lack peace with God. It might be habits of thought or behavior, relationships, or circumstances. With specificity acknowledge your guilt—what you have done wrong or left undone. Express your regret and sorrow, asking for God's strength to make things right, to apologize, or to make restitution where appropriate and to keep you from repeating these failures

in the future. Receive God's forgiveness and thank him for giving you his peace.

- Do a peace review each day. Just as coaches and athletes sometimes watch game-day videos so they can analyze and improve their skills, imagine you and Jesus are watching a video replay of the previous day. As you reflect on your morning, afternoon, and evening, consider two questions: *In what ways did I experience peace with God and others? In what ways did I fail to experience peace with God and others?* Use a pad of paper or a journal to note your observations. Prayerfully invite Jesus to coach you on how to pursue and experience greater peace with God and others in the day ahead.

Advent Hymn

O COME, O COME, EMMANUEL

O come, O come, Emmanuel,
And ransom captive Israel,
That mourns in lonely exile here
Until the Son of God appear.
Rejoice! Rejoice!
Emmanuel shall come to thee, O Israel.

O come, Thou Wisdom from on high,
Who orderest all things mightily;
To us the path of knowledge show,
And teach us in her ways to go.
Rejoice! Rejoice!
Emmanuel shall come to thee, O Israel.

O come, Thou Rod of Jesse, free
Thine own from Satan's tyranny;
From depths of hell Thy people save,
And give them victory over the grave.
Rejoice! Rejoice!
Emmanuel shall come to thee, O Israel.

O come, Thou Day-spring, come and cheer
Our spirits by Thine advent here;
Disperse the gloomy clouds of night,

And death's dark shadows put to flight.
Rejoice! Rejoice!
Emmanuel shall come to thee, O Israel.

O come, Thou Key of David, come,
And open wide our heavenly home;
Make safe the way that leads on high,
And close the path to misery.
Rejoice! Rejoice!
Emmanuel shall come to thee, O Israel.

O come, O come, great Lord of might,
Who to Thy tribes on Sinai's height
In ancient times once gave the law
In cloud and majesty and awe.
Rejoice! Rejoice!
Emmanuel shall come to thee, O Israel.

O come, Thou Root of Jesse's tree,
An ensign of Thy people be;
Before Thee rulers silent fall;
All peoples on Thy mercy call.
Rejoice! Rejoice!
Emmanuel shall come to thee, O Israel.

O come, Desire of nations, bind
In one the hearts of all mankind;

165

Bid Thou our sad divisions cease,
And be Thyself our King of Peace.
Rejoice! Rejoice!
Emmanuel shall come to thee, O Israel.

Lyrics: Traditional Hymn,
translated by John M. Neale, 1851

For a child is born to us, a son is given to us. . . . And
he will be called: Wonderful Counselor, Mighty God,
Everlasting Father, Prince of Peace.

Isaiah 9:6 NLT

Therefore, since we have been made right in God's sight
by faith, we have peace with God because of what Jesus
Christ our Lord has done for us. . . . and we confidently
and joyfully look forward to sharing God's glory.

Romans 5:1–2 NLT

God blesses those who work for peace, for they will be
called the children of God.

Matthew 5:9 NLT

Then Jesus said to her, "Your sins are forgiven. . . . go in peace."

Luke 7:48, 50

Peace [is] the rest of will that results from assurance about how things will turn out.

Dallas Willard, "Willard Words," dwillard.org

It is he who made us and not we ourselves, made us out of his peace to live in peace, out of his light to dwell in light, out of his love to be above all things loved and loving.

Frederick Buechner, *Secrets in the Dark*

Week 3: Joy

———⊷∞∞⊷———

Let there be jubilation,
celebration, and festivity!

O ur hope is sure, we have peace with God, and the Messiah is coming to set everything right in our sin-drenched world. Every tear will be dried, every hurting heart mended, every broken body healed, every torn relationship restored. We are treasured sons and daughters of the Most High God. The only reasonable response to God's lavish love and goodness is joy—pure joy!

Scripture
Psalm 126
Isaiah 61:1–4, 7–11
1 Thessalonians 5:16–24
Matthew 11:2–11

Questions for Reflection

1. Even when describing joy, the biblical writers never gloss over evil and suffering. The selected passages acknowledge a wide range of dark realities and conditions, among them:

Tears	Imprisonment	Every kind of evil
Weeping	Ashes	Blindness
Mourning	Ruins	Lameness
Grief	Devastations	Deafness
Poverty	Disgrace	Leprosy
Despair	Robbery	Death
Captivity	Wrongdoing	

Max described such unwelcome intrusions in our lives as "interruptions." And the impact? "They can stir fear and anxiety," he writes, "They steal our sleep and pickpocket our joy. They can cause us to question God, even turn away from God" (pages 35–36).

- Which words or phrases on the list come closest to describing a recent "interruption" you've experienced or one you're experiencing now?

- How has this interruption affected you? For example, consider the emotional, physical, relational, and financial consequences.
- Max characterizes Christmas as "a season of interruptions." In what ways, if any, does the holiday season complicate or intensify the effect of your interruptions? In what ways, if any, do the holidays lighten your burden?
- How would you describe your awareness and experience of God throughout this season? For example, does God seem especially close or distant? Do you find yourself turning toward God or away from him, or do you vacillate?

2. The psalmist used the images of seeds and harvest to describe the miracle of God gleaning joy from suffering (Ps. 126:5–6). Author and pastor Eugene Peterson summarized it this way: "All suffering, all pain, all emptiness, all disappointment is seed: sow it in God and he will, finally, bring a crop of joy from it."[1] It is the same resurrection truth the apostle Paul described in his first letter to the church at Corinth:

> What is sown is perishable, what is raised is imperishable. It is sown in dishonor, it is raised in glory. It is sown in weakness, it is raised in power. (1 Cor. 15:42–43 NRSV)

If we think of the hardships of this life as seeds, we have at least three options for what we do with them:

We can refuse to plant. We can cling to our hardships and to our lives as they are.

We can plant in God. We can surrender our hardships and our lives in faith, trusting that God can and will produce crops of joy and new life.

We can plant in something other than God. We can choose the shallow soil of distractions or self-defeating behaviors in hopes they will produce a crop of quick relief. As Max acknowledges, "We shop till we drop, drink till we can't think, work till we can't stop" (page 123).

- How do you relate to each of the three options? Which one best describes how you dealt with or are dealing with the situation(s) you identified in question 1?

- Max points us to Psalm 11:3 and an ancient question that echoes today: "When all that is good falls apart, what can good people do?" (NCV). What is falling apart in our world today? What is falling apart in your personal world? Enumerate some of the challenges facing humanity. What interruptions are threatening your personal peace? Answer Max's question: "What is the godly response to these unexpected mishaps and calamities of life?"

God has made a business of turning tragedy into triumph. In what ways do the lives of Joseph, Moses, Daniel, and Jesus challenge and encourage you? How can your own encounter with adversity move you closer to understanding the sufferings of Christ?

3. The psalmist rehearsed God's wonders from the *past* and concluded, "Yes, the LORD has done amazing things for us! What joy!" (Ps. 126:3 NLT). When the prophet Isaiah considered how God had already saved him and also looked forward to what God would do in the *future*, he responded, "I am overwhelmed with joy in the LORD my God!" (Isa. 61:10 NLT). When it came to joy, the apostle Paul said there is no time like the *present*: "Always be joyful" (1 Thess. 5:16 NLT). Joy is a time traveler. It constantly scans the timeline—from ancient history to infinity—and sets up camp on every occasion and every promise of God's lavish goodness.

- What brings you the greatest joy—remembering the past, experiencing the present, or anticipating the future? Which brings the least joy?

- Advent is a time-traveling season. There is joy in remembering God's gift of the Christ child, joy in celebrating God's presence with us now, and joy in anticipating the Second Advent. Which of these three sources of joy resonates most with you this Advent? Why?

Advent Prayer
Come, Lord Jesus. Be my joy.

Advent Practice
Consider using one or more of the following options to practice and experience joy this week.

- Plant a seed as an expression of trust that just as God will bring a plant from that seed, he will also bring a crop of joy from the seeds of every hardship you sow in him. For example, the bulbs of amaryllis flowers are often used as gifts during the Christmas season. The bulbs are typically sold in pots, grow well indoors, and need just a bit of sun and water to grow and bloom. But any seed will do, even grass seed! Follow the directions for planting and growing your seed(s) indoors, and allow the process of sowing, waiting, and growth to be a touchstone for your own reflections and growth in joy.
- Engage in "time travel" to search for joy. Use your journal or a notepad to create a three-column chart. At the top of the columns, write *Past*, *Present*, and *Future*. In each column write at least two or three ways in which you recognize God's lavish goodness to you—actions he has taken on your behalf. Then write down in each column any questions you have for God or any ways you are struggling to recognize God's goodness to you in that time period. Close with prayer, offering your chart

to God. Express your joy for his goodness to you and entrust your questions to him, asking to see the light of his goodness even in the dark places.

- As you reflect on the "interruption" of Jenna's miscarriage, ask God to remind you of a young couple experiencing a similar season of sadness. Pray for them, and ask God to show you how you might comfort and encourage them in the days ahead.

Advent Hymn

GOD REST YE MERRY, GENTLEMEN

God rest ye merry, gentlemen,
Let nothing you dismay,
Remember Christ our Savior
Was born on Christmas Day;
To save us all from Satan's power
When we were gone astray.
O tidings of comfort and joy, comfort and joy;
O tidings of comfort and joy.

In Bethlehem, in Israel,
This blessèd Babe was born,
And laid within a manger
Upon this blessèd morn;
The which His mother Mary
Did nothing take in scorn.
O tidings of comfort and joy, comfort and joy;
O tidings of comfort and joy.

From God our heavenly Father
A blessèd angel came;
And unto certain shepherds
Brought tidings of the same;
How that in Bethlehem was born
The Son of God by name.

O tidings of comfort and joy, comfort and joy;
O tidings of comfort and joy.

Fear not, then, said the angel,
Let nothing you affright
This day is born a Savior
Of a pure Virgin bright,
To free all those who trust in Him
From Satan's power and might.
O tidings of comfort and joy, comfort and joy;
O tidings of comfort and joy.

The shepherds at those tidings
Rejoiced much in mind,
And left their flocks a-feeding
In tempest, storm and wind,
And went to Bethl'em straightaway
This blessèd Babe to find.
O tidings of comfort and joy, comfort and joy;
O tidings of comfort and joy.

Now to the Lord sing praises
All you within this place,
And with true love and brotherhood
Each other now embrace;
This holy tide of Christmas
All others doth deface.

O tidings of comfort and joy, comfort and joy;
O tidings of comfort and joy.

Lyrics: Traditional English Carol

———❈———

You thrill me, LORD, with all you have done for me! I sing
for joy because of what you have done.

Psalm 92:4 NLT

———❈———

You make known to me the path of life; you will fill me
with joy in your presence, with eternal pleasures at your
right hand.

Psalm 16:11

———❈———

The joy of the LORD is your strength.

Nehemiah 8:10

———❈———

Joy has a history. Joy is the verified, repeated experience of
those involved in what God is doing.

Eugene H. Peterson, *A Long Obedience in the Same Direction*

———⟨∞⟩———

Joy is nurtured by anticipation. . . . Just as joy builds on the past, it borrows from the future. It expects certain things to happen.

Eugene H. Peterson, *A Long Obedience in the Same Direction*

———⟨∞⟩———

True joy, happiness, and inner peace come from the giving of ourselves to others. A happy life is a life for others.

Henri J. M. Nouwen, *Life of the Beloved*

Week 4: Love

———— ✇ ————

It really comes down to that:
God loves us.

"First we were loved," wrote the apostle John, "now we love" (1 John 4:19 MSG). God always takes the initiative—he blessed first, served first, comforted first, and most of all, loved first. And then it's up to us. How will we respond? At Advent, while much of the world around us is enamored by distractions and lesser loves, we seek to discover anew our first love, the love that "came down at Christmas,"[2] and then to share that love by blessing, serving, and comforting others.

Scripture
Psalm 89:1–4, 19–26
Micah 5:2–5a
Titus 3:3–8
Luke 1:39–55

Questions for Reflection

1. "The story of Christmas is the story of God's relentless love for us," Max writes, "Let him love you. . . . You might question his actions, decisions, or declarations. But you can never, ever question his zany, stunning, unquenchable affection" (pages 134–135).

   - As you reflect on your relationship with God, when would you say you were most aware and most certain of God's love for you? How, specifically, did you let God love you?

   - Even though God's love is always apparent, we go through seasons when we doubt it. What, if anything, has led you to question God's love for you?

   - Do you find it difficult to let God love you in your current season of life? Why or why not?

2. When it came to expressing the wonder of God's love, the psalmist couldn't help but break into song:

   I will sing of the LORD's great love forever;
   > with my mouth I will make your faithfulness known
   > through all generations.

I will declare that your love stands firm forever,
    that you have established your faithfulness in heaven
    itself. (Ps. 89:1–2)

This is a heart-wide-open declaration that reflects all
the fervency and devotion of a first love. The psalmist
essentially said to God, "Your loyal love is so amazing
that I will never stop singing about it!"

- Using temperature as a gauge, which of the following
  statements comes closest to describing your heart right
  now?
  - *Hot.* I am so amazed by God's love for me I can't
    help sharing it with others.
  - *Warm.* I am committed to my faith, but I'm not as
    passionate about God or as loving toward others as
    I should be.
  - *Cold.* I feel distant from or ambivalent about God.
  - *Other:*
- What connections could you make between the
  statement you just checked and your responses
  to question 1? In other words, how might your
  willingness to let God love you affect your ability to
  love God and others wholeheartedly?

3. The apostle Paul sought to rekindle in his readers
   the flames of love for God and others by reminding
   them about who they were before they received
   God's love:

We . . . were foolish, disobedient, deceived and enslaved by all kinds of passions and pleasures. We lived in malice and envy, being hated and hating one another. But when the kindness and love of God our Savior appeared, he saved us, not because of righteous things we had done, but because of his mercy. (Titus 3:3–5)

Jesus said, "A person who is forgiven little shows only little love" (Luke 7:47 NLT). Paul wanted his readers to show great love, so he reminded them of how much they had been forgiven. He then spelled out the implications of God's sacrificial love for us:

I want you to stress these things, so that those who have trusted in God may be careful to devote themselves to doing what is good. (Titus 3:8)

- What words or phrases come to mind when you consider who you were before you gave your life to Christ and received God's love? (If you find this difficult because you gave your life to Christ as a child, use the apostle Paul's description as a starting point and consider instead the darkness you were saved from because of your early relationship with God.)
- How does remembering who you were before Christ (or what Christ has saved you from) affect you? In what ways, if any, does it increase your awareness of your love for Christ?

4. Echoing the apostle Paul's teaching in the Titus passage, Max writes, "In the manger God loves you; through the cross God saves you. But has he taken you to his home? Not yet. He has work for you to do. He wants the world to see what God can do with his purchased possessions" (page 125).

- It has been said, "It is Christmas every time you let God love others through you." How have you recently experienced "Christmas" because God loved you through someone else?

- What words or phrases would characterize this person and his or her devotion to doing what is good (Titus 3:8)? Based on his or her example, how would you complete the following sentence in your own words? *Letting God love others through me means . . .*

- How would you describe the work that you sense God has for you to do right now, the ways in which he seems to be inviting you to do good and bring "Christmas" to others? Or, what do you hope God can do with you, his beloved possession?

Advent Prayer
Come, Lord Jesus. I love you.

Advent Practice
Consider using one or more of the following options to practice giving and receiving love this week.

- Focus your thoughts and daily prayers on your love relationship with God. At the beginning of each day, invite God to show you how he loves you. Drawing on the example of Psalm 89, tell God how much you love him, focusing not only on his good gifts to you but also on who he is—loving, patient, good, holy. Or if you struggle to express your love to God, tell him why, and ask for his help. Before the week is done, "go public," as the psalmist did, and share with at least one other person something you've learned about God's love for you or your love for God or an example of how God demonstrated his love for you this week. If you find it helpful, write down your daily prayers, your expressions of love to God, and your observations as you look expectantly each day for God to show you how he loves you.

- Author Glennon Doyle Melton wrote, "Every time we open our mouths and speak, we are either saying *let there be light* or *let there be darkness*."[3] In the spirit of Advent, show love this week by seeking to bring light with every word you speak. As a visual reminder, use the image of a star or a candle as the wallpaper on your laptop or phone, or place a few sticky notes around your home or workplace that say, "Speak light!" or "Let there be light!"

- Choose one relationship to focus on this week. It might be a spouse, a child, a parent, a coworker, a friend. Filter every interaction with this person through one question: What does love require of me in this moment? Then do it. Let love dictate your demeanor, your body language, your words, your actions. Use a notepad or a journal to write down your observations each day, recording any challenges or effect your commitment to love has on your relationship.

Advent Hymn

ANGELS FROM THE REALMS OF GLORY

Angels from the realms of glory,
Wing your flight o'er all the earth;
Ye who sang creation's story
Now proclaim Messiah's birth.
Come and worship, come and worship,
Worship Christ, the newborn king.

Shepherds, in the field abiding,
Watching o'er your flocks by night,
God with us is now residing;
Yonder shines the infant light:
Come and worship, come and worship,
Worship Christ, the newborn king.

Sages, leave your contemplations,
Brighter visions beam afar;
Seek the great Desire of nations;
Ye have seen His natal star.
Come and worship, come and worship,
Worship Christ, the newborn king.

Saints, before the altar bending,
Watching long in hope and fear;
Suddenly the Lord, descending,

In His temple shall appear.
Come and worship, come and worship,
Worship Christ, the newborn king.

Sinners, wrung with true repentance,
Doomed for guilt to endless pains,
Justice now revokes the sentence,
Mercy calls you; break your chains.
Come and worship, come and worship,
Worship Christ, the newborn king.

Though an Infant now we view Him,
He shall fill His Father's throne,
Gather all the nations to Him;
Every knee shall then bow down:
Come and worship, come and worship,
Worship Christ, the newborn king.

All creation, join in praising
God, the Father, Spirit, Son,
Evermore your voices raising
To th'eternal Three in One.
Come and worship, come and worship,
Worship Christ, the newborn king.

Lyrics: James Montgomery, 1816

189

See what great love the Father has lavished on us, that we should be called children of God! And that is what we are!

1 John 3:1

⸺ ⸰⸰⸰ ⸺

Regardless of what else you put on, wear love. It's your basic, all-purpose garment. Never be without it.

Colossians 3:14 MSG

⸺ ⸰⸰⸰ ⸺

[Jesus] does not call us to do what he did, but to be as he was, permeated with love. Then the doing of what he did and said becomes the natural expression of who we are in him.

Dallas Willard, *The Divine Conspiracy*

⸺ ⸰⸰⸰ ⸺

The heavenly Father cherishes the earth and each human being upon it. The fondness, the endearment, the unstintingly affectionate regard of God toward all his creatures is the natural outflow of what he is to the core—which we vainly try to capture with our tired but indispensable old word "love."

Dallas Willard, *The Divine Conspiracy*

———⚬⚬⚬———

Truly he taught us to love one another, his law is love and his gospel is peace.

Placide Cappeau, "O Holy Night"

———⚬⚬⚬———

Turn around and believe that the good news that we are loved is gooder than we ever dared hope, and that to believe in that good news, to live out of it and toward it, to be in love with that good news, is of all glad things in this world the gladdest thing of all.

Amen, and come, Lord Jesus.

Frederick Buechner, *The Clown in the Belfry*

Christmas Eve / Christmas Day

—⟨∞⟩—

God became one of us so we could
become one with him.

The joy and promise of Christmas is that the miracle of
Bethlehem still happens. God still enters into the reality
of our messy everyday lives and loves us. And so on this day,
we open wide our hearts to receive the Christ child with joy.

Scripture
Psalm 96
Isaiah 9:2–7
Hebrews 1:1–12
Luke 2:1–20

Questions for Reflection

1. Luke's account of Jesus' birth includes several characters and lots of action:

   Mary and Joseph undertake a long journey under adverse conditions.

   The Christ child is born in a humble stable.

   The angel of the Lord brings good news of great joy to the shepherds.

   The heavenly host praises God.

   The shepherds are initially afraid but then receive and share the good news.

   All who hear the good news are amazed.

   Mary treasures up and ponders all she has experienced.

   - As you read the passage from Luke 2, which characters or circumstances best represent you in your relationship with Jesus right now? For example, like Mary and Joseph, perhaps you find yourself in the midst of a difficult journey with Christ, seeking shelter and rest. Like the Christ child, you may be in humble or vulnerable circumstances, longing for comfort and care.

   - How does the character or circumstance you identified help you understand what you long for in your relationship with Christ?

2. Luke pointed out a compelling contrast when he noted that "all who heard it were *amazed*. . . . But Mary *treasured up* all these things and *pondered* them in her heart" (Luke 2:18–19, emphasis mine).

194

- To be amazed is to be astonished, surprised, or stunned. Depending on the circumstances, amazement might lead to admiration and wonder, or to shock and bewilderment. The contrast Luke identified between Mary and "all who . . . were amazed" doesn't suggest that Mary's response was better, but it was noticeably different. Based on your own experiences, how would you describe the difference between the two responses? What changes in you when you move from being amazed at an experience to treasuring or pondering that experience?
- The Greek words translated "treasured up" and "pondered," mean to keep safe and close, to protect and preserve in memory, to bring together in one's mind or to confer with oneself. During the four weeks of Advent, you've had a chance to reflect on many truths about the gifts we receive from Christ—hope, peace, joy, and love. As you reflect on this four-week journey, what insights or experiences—with God and others—do you want to treasure up? Briefly identify a few, and then allow yourself to ponder them in God's presence, thanking him for these gifts and inviting him to reveal to you something of himself through them.

3. Max writes, "If the King was willing to enter the world of animals and shepherds and swaddling clothes, don't you think he's willing to enter yours? He took on your face in the hope that you would see his" (page 20).

- As you anticipate not only your celebration of Christmas but also the days and weeks to come, in what circumstance or relationship do you feel the greatest need to see the face of Immanuel, God with you?
- "When Christ was born, so was our hope. . . . The manger . . . dares us to believe the best is yet to be. And it could all begin today" (page 135, 9). What is the best you might dare to believe about the circumstance or relationship you just identified? Prayerfully surrender these hopes to God, trusting that he is already at work to provide the light you seek, the help you need, the deliverance you long for.

Christmas Prayer

Welcome, Lord Jesus. Make my heart your home this day.

Christmas Practice

God created celebration: he is the author of joy, pleasure, and merriment. In fact, Jesus described the kingdom as a great banquet to which everyone is invited (Matt. 22:1–14). At Christmas we train our hearts for heaven by celebrating God's miraculous gift of Jesus. And just as Paul and Silas chose to sing praises even while imprisoned (Acts 16:22–25), we can choose joy and celebration at Christmas regardless of our circumstances. Author and pastor Adele Calhoun wrote:

The world is filled with reasons to be downcast. But deeper than sorrow thrums the unbroken pulse of God's joy, a joy that will yet have its eternal day. To set our hearts on this joy reminds us that we can choose how we respond to any particular moment. We can search for God in all circumstances, or not. We can seek the pulse of hope and celebration because it is God's reality. Heaven is celebrating. . . . Every small experience of Jesus with us is a taste of the joy that is to come. We are not alone—and that in itself is reason to celebrate.[4]

God invites you to choose joy this day, to follow the happy commands of the psalmist: *Sing! Praise! Proclaim! Declare! Worship!* (see Psalm 96). Max puts it this way:

For your own sake do what the angels did: make a big deal about the arrival of the King. . . . Do you love God? Let him know. Tell him! Out loud. In public. Unashamed. Let there be jubilation, celebration, and festivity! (page 65–66)

And you can choose joy in quiet ways as well. Be watchful for "every small experience of Jesus," knowing that he often shows up in unexpected ways. Treasure up and ponder all the ways Christ reveals himself to you—in events, music, meals, relationships, beauty, and the comfort of his presence with you.

Christmas Hymn

HARK! THE HERALD ANGELS SING

Hark! The herald angels sing,
Glory to the newborn King;
Peace on earth, and mercy mild,
God and sinners reconciled!

Joyful, all ye nations rise,
Join the triumph of the skies;
Nature rise and worship him,
Who is born in Bethlehem!

Christ, by highest Heav'n adored;
Christ the everlasting Lord;
Late in time, behold Him come,
Offspring of a virgin's womb.

Veiled in flesh the Godhead see;
Hail th'incarnate Deity,
Pleas'd as Man with Men t'appear,
Jesus our Emmanuel here.

Hail the Heav'n-born Prince of Peace
Hail the Son of Righteousness!
Light and Life around he brings,
Ris'n with Healing in his Wings.

Mild he lays his Glory by,
Born that Men no more may die;
Born to raise the Sons of Earth,
Born to give them second Birth.

Lyrics: Charles Wesley (1739) and George Whitefield (1753)

The Word became flesh and blood, and moved into the neighborhood.

John 1:14 MSG

I bring you good news that will bring great joy to all people. The Savior—yes, the Messiah, the Lord—has been born today in Bethlehem, the city of David!

Luke 2:10–11 NLT

For this is how God loved the world: He gave his one and only Son, so that everyone who believes in him will not perish but have eternal life.

John 3:16 NLT

You always get your Christmas miracle. You get God with you. . . .

Christ is all your good, and He is all yours, and this is always all your miracle.

No matter the barrenness you feel, you can always have as much of Jesus as you want.

Ann Voskamp, *The Greatest Gift*

───※───

The eternal Son became a child so that I might become a child again and so reenter with him into the Kingdom of the Father.

Henri J. M. Nouwen, *The Return of the Prodigal Son*

───※───

Who can add to Christmas? The perfect motive is that God so loved the world.

The perfect gift is that he gave his only Son.

The only requirement is to believe in him.

The reward of faith is that you shall have everlasting life.

attributed to Corrie ten Boom

Notes

Chapter 2: God Has a Face
1. Max Lucado, *God Came Near: Chronicles of the Christ* (Portland, OR: Multnomah, 1987).
2. John 11:1–36; Matthew 14:22–33; John 8:1–11.
3. Stephen Seamands, *Give Them Christ: Preaching His Incarnation, Crucifixion, Resurrection, Ascension and Return* (Downers Grove, IL: IVP Books, 2012), 38–40.

Chapter 3: Saved from Ourselves
1. Frederick Dale Bruner, *Matthew: A Commentary*, vol. 1, *The Christbook: Matthew 1–12*, rev. and exp. ed. (Grand Rapids: William B. Eerdmans, 2004), 29–30.

Chapter 6: Worship Works Wonders
1. Terry Wardle, *Exalt Him! Designing Dynamic Worship Services* (Camp Hill, PA: Christian Publications, 1992), 23.
2. "Always on My Mind," by Wayne Carson, Johnny Christopher, and Mark James, published 1972.

3. Matthew 12:34 NKJV.

4. John Wesley, *The Works of the Reverend John Wesley, A. M.* (New York: B. Waugh and T. Mason, 1835), 7:609.

5. Harold Boulton, "All Through the Night," http://www.carols.org.uk/a45-all-through-the-night.htm.

6. "Bertie Felstead," *The Economist*, August 2, 2001, http://www.economist.com/node/718781.

Chapter 7: God Guides the Wise

1. Frederick Dale Bruner, *Matthew: A Commentary*, vol. 1, *The Christbook: Matthew 1–12*, rev. and exp. ed. (Grand Rapids: William B. Eerdmans, 2004), 60.

2. "Water Scene," *The Miracle Worker*, directed by Paul Aaron (1979; Atlanta, GA: Half-Pint Productions).

Chapter 8: Humility Shines

1. Dean Farrar, *The Life of Christ* (London: Cassell, n.d.), 22–23.

2. Flavius Josephus, *The Works of Josephus*, updated ed., trans. William Whiston (Peabody, MA: Hendrickson, 1987), 882.

3. G. K. Chesterton, *Orthodoxy* (Hollywood, FL: Simon and Brown, 2012), 17.

4. *The International Standard Bible Encyclopedia*, ed., Geoffrey W. Bromiley, vol. 2, *E–J* (Grand Rapids: William B. Eerdmans, 1982), 693.

Chapter 9: Perhaps Today

1. Norval Geldenhuys, *Commentary on the Gospel of Luke: The English Text with Introduction, Exposition and Notes* (Grand Rapids: William B. Eerdmans, 1954), 117–18.

2. Dean Farrar, *The Life of Christ* (London: Cassell, n.d.), 40.
3. Walter L. Liefeld, "Luke," in *The Expositor's Bible Commentary*, ed. Frank E. Gaebelein (Grand Rapids: Zondervan, 1984), 8:849.
4. Edmund Sears, "That Glorious Song of Old," v. 2, public domain.

Chapter 10: Crown, Cradle, and Cross

1. "Whirlpool Galaxy Facts," Space Facts, http://space-facts.com/whirlpool-galaxy/.
2. Tim Sharp, "How Big Is the Sun?/Size of the Sun," Space.com, August 8, 2012, www.space.com/17001-how-big-is-the-sun-size-of-the-sun.html.
3. Space.com staff, "Supergiant Star's Rainbow Nebula Revealed," Space.com, June 23, 2011, http://www.space.com/12051-bright-nebula-photo-supergiant-star-betelgeuse.html.
4. Miriam Kramer, "Supergiant Star Betelgeuse to Crash into Cosmic 'Wall,'" Space.com, January 25, 2013, http://www.space.com/19415-supergiant-star-betelgeuse-crash-photo.html.
5. Extract by C S Lewis © copyright C S Lewis Pte Ltd. Used by permission.

Chapter 11: It's Good-Bye to the Bents

1. Rick Warren, *The Purpose of Christmas* (New York: Howard Books, 2008), 41.
2. John 4:4–29.
3. Mark 5:1–15.
4. Luke 19:1–10.

Chapter 12: Every Day a Christmas, Every Heart a Manger

1. Joseph F. Kelly, *The Birth of Christmas* (Waco, TX: Center for Christian Ethics at Baylor University, 2011), 15, http://www.baylor.edu/content/services/document.php/159119.pdf.
2. J. B. Phillips, *New Testament Christianity* (Eugene, OR: Wipf and Stock, 2012), 15–16.

Study Guide Sessions

1. Eugene H. Peterson, *A Long Obedience in the Same Direction: Discipleship in an Instant Society*, rev. and exp. ed. (Downer's Grove, IL: InterVarsity Press, 1980, 2000), 100.
2. Christina Rossetti, "Love Came Down at Christmas," All Poetry, http://allpoetry.com/Love-Came-Down-at-Christmas.
3. Glennon Doyle Melton, https://www.facebook.com/glennondoylemelton, Facebook post, April 12, 2015.
4. Adele Ahlberg Calhoun, *Spiritual Disciplines Handbook: Practices That Transform Us* (Downers Grove, IL: InterVarsity Press, 2005), 27.

IN THE
MANGER

For with God nothing will be impossible.

LUKE 1:37

INTRODUCTION

A small cathedral outside Bethlehem marks the supposed birthplace of Jesus. Behind a high altar in the church is a cave, a little cavern lit by silver lamps.

You can enter the main edifice and admire the ancient church. You can also enter the quiet cave, where a star embedded in the floor recognizes the birth of the King. There is one stipulation, however. You have to stoop. The door is so low you can't go in standing up.

The same is true of the Christ. You can see the world standing tall, but to witness the Savior, you have to get on your knees.

So at the birth of Jesus . . .

> while the theologians were sleeping
> and the elite were dreaming
> and the successful were snoring,
> the meek were kneeling.

They were kneeling before the One only the meek will see. They were kneeling in front of Jesus.

The Applause of Heaven

1

The Author
of Life

Then God said, "Let there be light."
GENESIS 1:3

Seated at the great desk, the Author opens the large book. It has no words because no words exist. No words exist because no words are needed. There are no ears to hear them, no eyes to read them. The Author is alone.

And so he takes the great pen and begins to write. Like an artist gathers his colors and a woodcarver his tools, the Author assembles his words.

There are three. Three single words. Out of these three will pour a million thoughts. But on these three words, the story will suspend.

He takes his quill and spells the first. *T-i-m-e.*

Time did not exist until he wrote it. He, himself, is timeless, but his story would be encased in time. The story would have a first rising of the sun, a first shifting of the sand. A beginning . . . and an end. A final chapter. He knows it before he writes it.

Time. A footspan on eternity's trail.

Slowly, tenderly, the Author writes the second word. A name. *A-d-a-m.*

As he writes, he sees him, the first Adam. Then he sees all the others. In a thousand eras in a thousand lands, the Author sees them. Each Adam. Each child. Instantly loved. Permanently loved. To each he assigns a time and appoints a place. No accidents. No coincidences. Just design.

The Author makes a promise to these unborn: *In my image, I will make you. You will be like me. You will laugh. You will create. You will never die. And you will write.*

They must. For each life is a book, not to be read, but rather a story to be written. The Author starts each life story, but each life will write his or her own ending.

What a dangerous liberty. How much safer it would have been to finish the story for each Adam. To script every option. It would have been simpler and safer. But it would not have been love. Love is only love if chosen.

So the Author decides to give each child a pen. "Write carefully," he writes.

Lovingly, deliberately, he writes a third word, already feeling the pain. *I-m-m-a-n-u-e-l.*

The greatest mind in the universe imagined time. The truest judge granted Adam a choice. But it was love that gave Immanuel, *God with us.*

The Author would enter his own story. The Word

would become flesh. He, too, would be born. He, too, would be human. He, too, would have feet and hands, tears and flesh.

And most importantly, he, too, would have a choice. Immanuel would stand at the crossroads of life and death and make a choice.

The Author knows well the weight of the decision. He pauses as he writes the page of his own pain. He could stop. Even the Author has a choice. But how can Love not love? So he chooses life, though it means death, with hope that his children will do the same.

And so the Author of Life completes the story. He drives the spike in the flesh and rolls the stone over the grave. Knowing the choice he will make, knowing the choice all Adams will make, he pens, "The End," then closes the book and proclaims the beginning.

"Let there be light!"

A Gentle Thunder

O Lord, Author of my life, thank you for creating me in your image and starting my story. Help me write it carefully and truly become like you. Come, O come, Immanuel, and help me complete my story well. In Jesus' name, amen.

2

Why Would He Come?

Christ himself was like God in everything.... But he gave up his place with God and made himself nothing. He was born as a man and became like a servant.

Philippians 2:6–7 NCV

hy? Why did Jesus travel so far?

I was asking myself that question when I spotted the squirrels outside my window. A family of black-tailed squirrels had made its home amid the roots of the tree north of my office. They watch me peck the keyboard. I watch them store their nuts and climb the trunk. We're mutually amused.

But I've never considered becoming one of them. The squirrel world holds no appeal to me. Give up the Rocky Mountains, bass fishing, weddings, and laughter for a hole in the ground and dirty nuts? Count me out.

But count Jesus in. What a world he left. Our classiest mansion would be a tree trunk to him. Earth's finest cuisine would be walnuts on heaven's table. And the idea of becoming a squirrel with claws and a furry tail? It's nothing compared to God becoming a one-celled embryo and entering the womb of Mary.

But he did. The God of the universe was born into the poverty of a peasant and spent his first night in the cow's feed trough. The God of the universe left the glory of heaven and moved into our neighborhood. Who could have imagined he would do such a thing?

Why? He loves to be with the ones he loves.

Dr. Maxwell Maltz tells a remarkable story of a love like this. A man had been burned and disfigured in a fire while attempting to save his parents from a burning house, but he couldn't get to them. They perished. He mistakenly interpreted his pain as God's punishment. The man would not let anyone see him—not even his wife.

She went to Dr. Maltz, a plastic surgeon, for help. He told her not to worry. "I can restore his face."

The wife was unenthused. Her husband had repeatedly refused any help. She knew he would again.

Then why her visit? "I want you to disfigure my face so I can be like him! If I can share his pain, maybe he'll let me back in his life."

Dr. Maltz was shocked. He denied her request but was so moved by her love that he went to speak with her husband. Knocking on the man's bedroom door, he called loudly. "I'm a plastic surgeon, and I can restore your face." No response. "Please come out." Again there was no answer.

Still speaking through the door, Dr. Maltz told the man of his wife's proposal. "She wants me to disfigure her face, to make her face like yours in the hope that you let her back into your life. That's how much she loves you."

There was a brief moment of silence, and then, ever so slowly, the doorknob began to turn.

The way the woman felt for her husband is the way God feels about us. But he did more than make the offer. He took on our face, our disfigurement. He became like us. Just look at the places he was willing to go: feed troughs, carpentry shops, badlands, and cemeteries. The places he went to reach us show how far he will go to touch us.

He loves to be with the ones he loves.

Next Door Savior

Great God of the universe, I am amazed that you would leave the glory of heaven and become like me. I come to you with my disfigurement and ask you to touch me with your love. I want to be with you as well. In Jesus' name, amen.

3

Just Call
Him "Jesus"

Behold, the virgin shall conceive and bear a
Son, and shall call His name Immanuel.

Isaiah 7:14

It was about to begin—God's plan for humanity, crafted in the halls of heaven and carried out on the plains of earth. Only holiness could have imagined it. Only divinity could have enacted it. Only righteousness could have endured it.

And once the plan began, there would be no turning back. The Creator knew it. The Son knew it. And soon, earth itself would witness heaven's majesty alighting on the planet.

When God chose to reveal himself to mankind, what medium did he use? A book? No, that was secondary. A church? No, that was consequential. A moral code? No. To limit God's revelation to a cold list of dos and don'ts is as tragic as looking at a Colorado road map and saying that you'd seen the Rockies.

When God chose to reveal himself, he did so through a human body. The hand that touched the leper had dirt under its nails. The feet upon which the woman wept were calloused and dusty. And his tears . . . oh, don't miss the tears . . . they came from a heart as broken as yours or mine ever has been.

So, people came to him. My, how they came to him!

They came at night; they touched him as he walked down the street; they followed him around the sea; they invited him into their homes and placed their children at his feet. Why? Because he refused to be a statue in a cathedral or a priest in an elevated pulpit. He chose instead to be Jesus.

There was not a hint of one person who was afraid to draw near him. There were those who mocked him, were envious of him, and misunderstood him. There were those who revered him. But no one considered him too holy or too divine to touch.

There was not one person who was reluctant to approach him for fear of being rejected.

Remember that the next time you find yourself amazed at your own failures.

Or the next time acidic accusations burn holes in your soul.

Or the next time you see a cold cathedral or hear a lifeless liturgy.

Remember. It is man who creates the distance. It is Jesus who builds the bridge.

God Came Near

Loving Father, thank you for sending your Son and revealing your broken heart and tears. I welcome your invitation to call your Son, Jesus, my Savior. Despite my failures, I draw near to you without fear because of your love. In Jesus' name, amen.

4

GOD CAME NEAR

For unto us a Child is born, unto us a Son is given;
and the government will be upon His shoulder. And
His name will be called Wonderful, Counselor,
Mighty God, Everlasting Father, Prince of Peace.

ISAIAH 9:6

It all happened in a moment, a most remarkable moment.

As moments go, that one appeared no different than any other. It came and it went. It was one of the countless moments that have marked time since eternity became measurable.

But in reality, that particular moment was like none other. For through that segment of time a spectacular thing occurred. God became a man. While the creatures of earth walked unaware, Divinity arrived. Heaven opened herself and placed her most precious one in a human womb.

The omnipotent, in one instant, made himself breakable. He who had been spirit became pierceable. He who was larger than the universe became an embryo. And he who sustains the world with a word chose to be dependent upon the nourishment of a young girl.

God as a fetus. Holiness sleeping in a womb. The Creator of life being created.

God was given eyebrows, elbows, two kidneys, and a spleen. He stretched against the walls and floated in the amniotic fluid of his mother.

God came near.

He came, not as a flash of light or as an unapproach-able conqueror, but as one whose first cries were heard by a peasant girl and a sleepy carpenter. The hands that first held him were unmanicured, calloused, and dirty.

No silk. No ivory. No hype. No party. No hoopla.

Were it not for the shepherds, there would have been no reception. And were it not for a group of stargazers, there would have been no gifts.

Angels watched as Mary changed God's diaper. Children played in the street with him. He may have had pimples and been tone-deaf. Perhaps a girl down the street had a crush on him or vice versa. One thing's for sure: he was, while completely divine, completely human.

For thirty-three years he would feel everything you and I have ever felt. He felt weak. He grew weary. He was afraid of failure. He was susceptible to wooing women. He got colds, burped, and had body odor. His feelings got hurt. And his head ached.

To think of Jesus in such a light seems almost irrever-ent, doesn't it? It's uncomfortable. It is much easier to keep the humanity out of the incarnation. There is something about keeping him divine that keeps him distant, packaged, predictable.

But don't do it. For heaven's sake, don't. Let him be as human as he intended to be. Let him into the mire and muck of our world. For only if we let him in can he pull us out.

It all happened in one moment . . . a most remarkable moment. The Word became flesh.

There will be another. The world will see another instantaneous transformation. You see, in becoming man, God made it possible for man to see God. When Jesus went home he left the back door open. As a result, "we will all be changed—in a flash, in the twinkling of an eye" (1 Corinthians 15:51–52 NIV).

The first moment of transformation went unnoticed by the world. But you can bet your sweet September that the second won't. The next time you use the phrase "just a moment," remember that's all the time it will take to change this world.

God Came Near

Dear Lord, it's impossible for me to fathom what it meant for you to take on human flesh and live as a man. Nevertheless, I believe in you. Help me to hope for even more—that one great day soon I'll see you and be changed forever! In Jesus' name, amen.

5

WITH GOD NOTHING IS IMPOSSIBLE

Then the angel said to her, "Do not be afraid,
Mary, for you have found favor with God. And
behold, you will conceive in your womb and bring
forth a Son, and shall call His name Jesus."

LUKE 1:30–31

Gabriel must have scratched his head at this one. He wasn't one to question his God-given missions. Sending fire and dividing seas were all in an eternity's work for this angel. When God sent, Gabriel went.

And when word got out that God was to become a man, Gabriel was enthused. He could envision the moment:

The Messiah in a blazing chariot.
The King descending on a fiery cloud.
An explosion of light from which the Messiah
would emerge.

That's what he expected. What he never expected, however, was a slip of paper with a Nazarene address. "God will become a baby," it read. "Tell the mother to name the child Jesus. And tell her not to be afraid."

Gabriel was never one to question, but this time he had to wonder.

God will become a baby? Gabriel remembered what baby Moses looked like. *That's okay for humans. But God?*

The heavens can't contain him; how could a body? Besides, have you seen what comes out of those babies? Hardly befitting for the Creator of the universe. To imagine a mother burping God on her shoulder—why, that was beyond what even an angel could imagine.

And what of this name—*Jesus*? Such a common name. There's a Jesus in every cul-de-sac. Come on, even *Gabriel* had more punch to it than *Jesus*. Call the baby *Eminence* or *Majesty* or *Heaven-sent*. Anything but *Jesus*.

So Gabriel scratched his head. But he had his orders. Take the message to Mary.

Must be a special girl, he assumed as he traveled. But one peek told him Mary was no queen. The mother-to-be of God was not regal. She was a Jewish peasant who'd barely outgrown her acne and had a crush on a guy named Joe.

And speaking of Joe—what does this fellow know? He's a carpenter. Look at him over there, sawdust in his beard and nail apron around his waist. You're telling me God is going to have dinner every night with a common laborer and call this guy "Dad"?

It was all Gabriel could do to keep from turning back.

———

"This is a peculiar idea you have, God," he must have muttered to himself.

Only heaven knows how long Gabriel fluttered unseen above Mary before he took a breath and broke the news. But he did. He told her the name, the plan, and not to be afraid. And when he announced, "With God nothing is impossible!" he said it as much for himself as for her.

For even though he couldn't answer the questions, he knew who could, and that was enough. And even though we can't answer them all, taking time to ask a few could be a good start.

When God Whispers Your Name

Gracious Father, the wonder of the good news of Jesus' coming as a baby never grows old. And it never will throughout eternity. You were the God of the impossible then and now. May your word be powerful within me, giving me strength to believe great things. In Jesus' name, amen.

6

WHO WOULD BELIEVE IT?

An angel of the Lord appeared to him in a dream,
saying, "Joseph, son of David, do not be afraid
to take to you Mary your wife, for that which
is conceived in her is of the Holy Spirit."

MATTHEW 1:20

Matthew describes Jesus' earthly father as a craftsman (Matthew 13:55). A small-town carpenter, he lives in Nazareth: a single-camel map dot on the edge of boredom. Is he the right choice? Doesn't God have better options? An eloquent priest from Jerusalem or a scholar from the Pharisees?

Why Joseph? A major part of the answer lies in his reputation: he gives it up for Jesus. "Then Joseph [Mary's] husband, being a just man, and not wanting to make her a public example, was minded to put her away secretly" (Matthew 1:19).

With the phrase "a just man," Matthew recognizes the status of Joseph. Nazareth viewed him as we might view an elder, deacon, or Bible class teacher. Joseph likely took pride in his standing, but Mary's announcement jeopardized it. *I'm pregnant.*

Now what? His fiancée is blemished, tainted . . . he is righteous, godly. On the one hand, he has the law. On the other hand, he has his love. The law says, stone her. Love says, forgive her. Joseph is caught in the middle.

Then comes the angel. Mary's growing belly gives no cause for concern, but reason to rejoice. "She carries the

Son of God in her womb," the angel announces. But who would believe it?

A bead of sweat forms beneath Joseph's beard. He faces a dilemma. Make up a lie and preserve his place in the community, or tell the truth and kiss his reputation good-bye. He makes his decision. "Joseph . . . took to him his wife, and did not know her till she had brought forth her firstborn Son" (Matthew 1:24–25).

Joseph swapped his Torah studies for a pregnant fiancée and an illegitimate son and made the big decision of discipleship. He placed God's plan ahead of his own.

3:16

Dear Lord, help me see your hand in life's bewil-
dering twists and knots. Speak to me so I'll
understand your way when I find myself trapped
in a hard place. Shine your light down upon me so
I can follow you. In Jesus' name, amen.

7

CHRIST IN YOU

"Let it be to me according to your word."

LUKE 1:38

What must it have been like for Mary to carry God in her womb?

The virgin birth is much more than a Christmas story; it is a picture of how close Christ will come to you. The first stop on his itinerary was a womb. Where will God go to touch the world? Look deep within Mary for an answer.

Better still, look deep within yourself. What he did with Mary, he offers to us! He issues a Mary-level invitation to all his children. "If you'll let me, I'll move in!"

Proliferating throughout Scripture is a preposition that leaves no doubt—the preposition *in*. Jesus lives *in* his children.

To his apostles, Christ declared, "I am *in* you" (John 14:20 NCV, emphasis mine).

Paul's prayer for the Ephesians was "that Christ may dwell *in* your hearts through faith" (Ephesians 3:17, emphasis mine).

"Christ *in* you, the hope of glory" (Colossians 1:27, emphasis mine).

And the sweetest invitation from Christ? "Here I am! I stand at the door and knock. If anyone hears my voice and opens the door, I will come *in* and eat with him, and he with me" (Revelation 3:20 NIV, emphasis mine).

Christ grew in Mary until he had to come out. Christ will grow in you until the same occurs. He will come out in your speech, in your actions, in your decisions. Every place you live will be a Bethlehem, and every day you live will be a Christmas. You, like Mary, will deliver Christ into the world.

God *in* us! Have we sounded the depth of this promise?

You are a modern-day Mary. Even more so. He was a fetus in her, but he is a force in you. He will do what you cannot do. Imagine a million dollars being deposited into your checking account. To any observer you look the same, except for the goofy smile, but are you? Not at all! With God *in* you, you have a million resources that you did not have before.

Can't stop drinking or worrying? Christ can. And he lives with*in* you.

Can't forgive the jerk, forget the past, or forsake your bad habits? Christ can! And he lives *in* you.

Paul knew this. "To this end I also labor, striving

according to His working which works *in* me mightily" (Colossians 1:29, emphasis mine).

Like Mary, you and I are indwelt by Christ. Find that hard to believe? How much more did Mary? The line beneath her picture in the high school annual did not read, "Aspires to be the mother of God." No. No one was more surprised by this miracle than she was.

And no one was more passive than she was. God did everything. Mary didn't volunteer to help. What did she have to offer? Advice? "From my perspective, a heavenly choir would add a nice touch." Yeah, right. She offered no assistance.

And she offered no resistance. She could have said, "Who am I to have God in my womb? I'm not enough." Or, "I've got other plans. I don't have time for God in my life."

Instead, Mary said, "Behold the maidservant of the Lord! Let it be to me according to your word" (Luke 1:38). If she is our measure, God seems less interested in talent and more interested in trust.

Unlike her, we tend to assist God, assuming our part is as important as his. Or we resist, thinking we are too bad or too busy. Yet when we assist or resist, we miss God's great grace. We miss out on the reason we were placed on earth—to be so pregnant with heaven's child that he lives through us. To be so full of him that we could say with Paul, "It is no longer I who live, but Christ lives in me" (Galatians 2:20).

Next Door Savior

O Lord, live in me. May your love beat in and through my heart. May you speak through my voice. Jesus, be the strength of my soul and the fire that purges wrongs from my desires. Fill me with your great abounding grace. In Jesus' name, amen.

8

CONCEIVED BY THE HOLY SPIRIT

Now the birth of Jesus Christ was as follows: After His mother Mary was betrothed to Joseph, before they came together, she was found with child of the Holy Spirit.

MATTHEW 1:18

J oseph was perched firmly on his branch in the tree. It was thick, reliable, and perfect for sitting. It was so strong that he didn't tremble when the storms came or the winds blew. No, this branch was predictable and solid and Joseph had no intention of leaving it.

That is, until he was told to go out on a limb.

As he sat securely on his branch, he looked up at the limb God wanted him to climb. He'd never seen one so thin! "There's no place to sit!" he said to himself. "There's no protection from the weather. And how could you sleep dangling from that quivering twig?"

Common sense told him not to go out on the limb. "Conceived by the Holy Spirit? Come on!"

Self-defense told him not to do it. "Who will believe me? What will our families think?"

Convenience told him not to do it. "Just when I was hoping to settle down and raise a family."

Pride told him not to do it. "If she expects me to buy a tale like that . . ."

But God told him to do it. And that's what bothered him.

It bothered him because he was happy where he was.

Life next to the tree trunk was good. His branch was big enough to allow him to sit in comfort. He was near scores of other branch-sitters and had made some valid contributions to the tree community. Surely God wouldn't want him to leave. He had roots here.

I have a feeling you can relate to Joseph. You've been there. You know the imbalance of having one foot in your will and one foot in his. Maybe you're in the midst of a decision. It's disrupting, isn't it? You've grown accustomed to your branch. And, like Joseph, you've been a pretty good branch-sitter. And then you hear the call. "I need you to go out on the limb and . . . take a moral stand . . . forgive . . . sacrifice."

Regardless of the nature of the call, the consequences are the same: civil war. Though your heart may say yes, your feet say no. Excuses blow as numerously as golden leaves in an autumn wind. "That's not my talent." "It's time for someone else to take charge." "Not now. I'll get to it tomorrow."

But eventually you're left staring at a bare tree and a hard choice: His will or yours?

Joseph chose God's. After all, it was really the only

option. Joseph knew that the only thing worse than a venture into the unknown was the thought of denying his Master. So, resolute, he grasped the smaller limb. With tight lips and a determined glint in his eye, he placed one hand in front of the other until he dangled in the air with only his faith in God as a safety net.

As things turned out, Joseph's fears were justified. Life wasn't as comfortable as it had been. The Messiah was to be born to Mary and raised in his home. He had to push away the sheep so his wife would have a place to give birth. He became a fugitive from the law. He spent two years trying to understand Egyptian.

Have you been called to go out on a limb for God? You can bet it won't be easy. Limb-climbing has never been easy. Ask Joseph. Or, better yet, ask Jesus.

He knows better than anyone the cost of hanging on a tree.

God Came Near

Heavenly Father, I see in Joseph's life the importance of responding to your call. Help me to be like him and to have the courage to go out on the limb you are calling me to. Strengthen my faith to believe you will always be there to support me. In Jesus' name, amen.

9

PACING
OUTSIDE
THE STABLE

Joseph also went up from Galilee, out of the city of
Nazareth, into Judea, to the city of David, which is called
Bethlehem, because he was of the house and lineage of
David, to be registered with Mary, his betrothed wife,
who was with child. So it was, that while they were
there, the days were completed for her to be delivered.

LUKE 2:4–6

The white space between Bible verses is fertile soil for questions. One can hardly read Scripture without whispering, "I wonder . . ."

The innkeeper too busy to welcome God—did he ever learn who he turned away? The shepherds—did they ever hum the song the angels sang? The wise men who followed the star—what was it like to worship a toddler?

And Joseph—did he ever look up from his prayers and see Jesus listening? Whatever happened to him?

His role in Act I is so crucial that we expect to see the rest of the drama—but with the exception of a short scene with twelve-year-old Jesus in Jerusalem, he never reappears. And we are left with our questions.

My first question would be about the night in the stable. Moonlit pastures. Stars twinkle above. Bethlehem sparkles in the distance. I picture Joseph there, pacing outside the stable.

He'd done all he could do to prepare as comfortable a place for Mary as he could in a barn, and then he stepped out. She'd asked to be alone, and Joseph has never felt more so.

In that eternity between his wife's dismissal and

Jesus' arrival, what was he thinking? I wonder if he said . . .

This isn't the way I planned it, God. Not at all. My child being born in a cave with sheep and donkeys? My wife giving birth with only the stars to hear her pain?

This isn't what I imagined. No, I imagined family, grandmothers, and neighbors clustered outside the door and friends standing at my side. I imagined the house erupting with the first cry of the infant. Slaps on the back. Loud laughter. Jubilation.

But now look. Here we are in a . . . sheep pasture. Who will celebrate with us?

Did I miss something, God?

When you sent the angel and spoke of the son being born, I envisioned Jerusalem, the temple, the priest, and the people gathered to watch. A pageant perhaps. A parade. A banquet at least. I mean, this is the Messiah?

This is not the way I wanted it to be for my son.

Oh my, I did it again, didn't I, Father? I don't

mean to do that; it's just that I forget. He's not my son . . . he's yours.

The child is yours. The plan is yours. The idea is yours. And forgive me for asking but . . . is this how God enters the world? The coming of the angel, I accepted. The questions people asked about the pregnancy, I can tolerate. The trip to Bethlehem, fine. But why a birth in a stable, God?

Any minute now Mary will give birth. Not to a child, but to the Messiah. Not to an infant, but to God. That's what the angel said. That's what Mary believes. And God, my God, that's what I want to believe. But surely you can understand, it's not easy.

He Still Moves Stones

Gracious Father, your ways are so far above our ways that our wildest imaginations can't begin to conceive your plans. I celebrate the wonder of the birth of your Son, and I bow my heart to what you want to do in and through my life. In Jesus' name, amen.

10

SEARCHING the NIGHT for a LIGHT

*So all this was done that it might be fulfilled which was
spoken by the Lord through the prophet, saying: "Behold, the
virgin shall be with child, and bear a Son, and they shall call
His name Immanuel," which is translated, "God with us."*

MATTHEW 1:22–23

On the night when Jesus was born, I wonder if Joseph ever prayed, "Father, this all seems so . . . bizarre. The angel you sent? Any chance you could send another? If not an angel, maybe a person? Some company would be nice. Even a shepherd would do."

Perhaps he did. Perhaps he didn't. But you probably have.

You've stood where Joseph stood. Caught between what God says and what makes sense. You've done what he told you to do only to wonder if it was him speaking in the first place. You've stared into a sky blackened with doubt. And you've asked what Joseph asked.

You've asked if you're still on the right road. You've asked if you were supposed to turn left when you turned right. And you've asked if there is a plan behind this scheme. Things haven't turned out as you thought they would.

Each of us knows what it's like to search the night for a light. Not outside a stable, but perhaps outside an emergency room or on the manicured grass of a cemetery. We've asked our questions. We've questioned

God's plan. And we've wondered why God does what he does.

The Bethlehem sky was not the first to hear the pleadings of a confused pilgrim.

If you are asking what Joseph asked, let me urge you to do what Joseph did. Obey. That's what he did. He obeyed when the angel called, when Mary explained, and when God sent.

He was obedient when the sky was bright . . . and when it was dark.

He didn't let his confusion disrupt his obedience. He didn't know everything. But he did what he knew. He shut down his business, packed up his family, and went to another country. Why? Because that's what God said to do.

What about you? Just like Joseph, you can't see the whole picture. Just like Joseph, your task is to see that Jesus is brought into your part of the world. And just like Joseph, you have a choice: to obey or disobey. Because Joseph obeyed, God used him to change the world.

Can he do the same with you?

God still looks for Josephs today. Men and women

who believe that God is not through with this world. Common people who serve an uncommon God.

Will you be that kind of person? Will you serve . . . even when you don't understand?

No, the Bethlehem sky was not the last to hear the pleadings of an honest heart. And perhaps God didn't answer every question for Joseph. But he answered the most important one. "Are you still with me, God?" And through the first cries of the God-child the answer came.

"Yes, Joseph. I'm with you."

Through the small face of the stable-born baby, he says yes.

Yes, your sins are forgiven.

Yes, your name is written in heaven.

Yes, death has been defeated.

And yes, God has entered your world.

Immanuel. God is with us.

He Still Moves Stones

Father, I've faced some dark nights of confusion, and I know there'll be more. Thank you that Jesus was born and you found a way to reach me in my lostness. Help me to always see you and obey you, especially when it's darkest. In Jesus' name, amen.

11

GOD DANCES amid THE COMMON

Now there were in the same country shepherds living out
in the fields, keeping watch over their flock by night. And
behold, an angel of the Lord stood before them, and the glory
of the Lord shone around them, and they were greatly afraid.

LUKE 2:8–9

There is one word that describes the night he came—ordinary.

The sky was ordinary. An occasional gust stirred the leaves and chilled the air. The stars were diamonds sparkling on black velvet. Fleets of clouds floated in front of the moon.

It was a beautiful night—a night worth peeking out your bedroom window to admire—but not really an unusual one. Nothing to keep a person awake. An ordinary night with an ordinary sky.

The sheep were ordinary. Some fat. Some scrawny. Some with barrel bellies. Some with twig legs. Common animals. No fleece made of gold. No blue-ribbon winners. They were simply sheep—lumpy, sleeping silhouettes on a hillside.

And the shepherds. Peasants they were. Probably wearing all the clothes they owned. Smelling like sheep and looking just as woolly. They were conscientious, willing to spend the night with their flocks. But you won't find their staffs in a museum or their writings in a library. No one asked their opinion on social justice or the application of the Torah. They were nameless and simple.

An ordinary night with ordinary sheep and ordinary shepherds. And were it not for a God who loves to hook an "extra" on the front of the ordinary, the night would have gone unnoticed. The sheep and shepherds would have been forgotten.

But God dances amid the common. And that night he did a waltz.

The black sky exploded with brightness. Trees that had been shadows jumped into clarity. Sheep that had been silent became a chorus of curiosity. One minute the shepherd was dead asleep; the next he was rubbing his eyes and staring into the face of an alien.

The night was ordinary no more.

The announcement went first to the shepherds. They didn't ask God if he was sure he knew what he was doing. Had the angel gone to theologians, they would have first consulted their commentaries. Had he gone to the elite, they would have looked around to see if anyone was watching. Had he gone to the successful, they would have first looked to their calendars.

So the angels went to the shepherds. Men who didn't have a reputation to protect or an ax to grind or a ladder to climb. Men who didn't know enough to tell God that angels don't sing to sheep and that messiahs aren't found sleeping in a feed trough.

The angels came in the night because that is when lights are best seen and that is when they are most needed. God comes into the common for the same reason.

His most powerful tools are the simplest.

The Applause of Heaven

O Lord, I rejoice that you are the uncommon God who comes to ordinary people like me. As the shepherds did, I simply welcome you to transform my life into the extraordinary by your grace and love. Come and dance with me. In Jesus' name, amen.

12

LINGER NEAR THE MANGER

Then the angel said to them, "Do not be afraid, for behold, I bring you good tidings of great joy which will be to all people. For there is born to you this day in the city of David a Savior, who is Christ the Lord."

LUKE 2:10–11

God tapped humanity on its collective shoulder. "Pardon me," he said, and eternity interrupted time, divinity interrupted carnality, and heaven interrupted the earth in the form of a baby. Christianity was born in one big heavenly interruption.

Just ask the Bethlehem shepherds. We know so little about these men. Their names? Their ages? How many were on duty that night? We don't know. But this much we can safely assume: they had no expectations of excitement. These are sheep they are watching. We count sheep to go to sleep!

Besides, this is the night shift. Might as well watch paint dry. Shepherds watching sheep sleep? Saying that sentence is more exciting than doing their job. Their greatest challenge was staying awake! These men expected no excitement.

Nor did they want any. Any excitement was bad excitement—wolves, mountain lions, poachers. Shepherds treasured the predictable. They coveted the calm. Their singular aim was to be able to tell their wives, "Nothing happened last night."

Just because they wanted a calm night, however, didn't mean they would get it.

"Then an angel of the Lord stood before them. The glory of the Lord was shining around them, and they became very frightened" (Luke 2:9 NCV).

Change always brings fear before it brings faith. We always assume the worst before we look for the best. God interrupts our lives with something we've never seen, and rather than praise, we panic! We interpret the presence of a problem as the absence of God and scoot!

Good thing the shepherds lingered. Otherwise they might have missed the second verse.

"Today your Savior was born in the town of David. He is Christ, the Lord" (Luke 2:11 NCV).

I hope you'll do what the shepherds did—linger near the manger.

God Came Near

My Lord and Savior, I'd like to join the shepherds and see your glory, hear your angels, and know you as you really are. Open the eyes of my heart that I may behold you in your Word. I want to linger near you and know you completely. In Jesus' name, amen.

13

THE FACE OF THE INFANT-GOD

And suddenly there was with the angel a multitude of the heavenly host praising God and saying: "Glory to God in the highest, and on earth peace, goodwill toward men!"

LUKE 2:13–14

Were someone to chance upon the sheep stable on the outskirts of Bethlehem that morning, what a peculiar scene they would behold.

The stable stinks as all stables do. The stench of urine, dung, and sheep reeks pungently in the air. The ground is hard, the hay scarce. Cobwebs cling to the ceiling and a mouse scurries across the dirt floor.

A more lowly place of birth could not exist.

Off to one side a group of shepherds sits silently on the floor; perhaps perplexed, perhaps in awe, no doubt in amazement. Their night watch had been interrupted by an explosion of light from heaven and a symphony of angels. God goes to those who have time to hear him—so on this night he went to simple shepherds.

Near the young mother sits the weary father. If anyone is dozing, he is. He can't remember the last time he sat down. And now that Mary and the baby are comfortable, he leans against the wall of the stable and feels his eyes grow heavy. The mystery of the event puzzles him. But he hasn't the energy to wrestle with the questions. What's important is that the baby is fine and that Mary is safe. As sleep comes, he remembers the name the angel told him to use . . . Jesus.

Wide awake is Mary. My, how young she looks! Her head rests on the soft leather of Joseph's saddle. The pain has been eclipsed by wonder. She looks into the face of the baby. Her son. Her Lord. His Majesty. At this point in history, the human being who best understands who God is and what he is doing is a teenage girl in a smelly stable. She can't take her eyes off him. Somehow Mary knows she is holding God. *So this is he.* She remembers the words of the angel. "Of His kingdom there will be no end" (Luke 1:33).

He looks like anything but a king. His face is prunish and red. His cry, though strong and healthy, is still the helpless and piercing cry of a baby. And he is absolutely dependent upon Mary for his well-being.

Majesty in the midst of the mundane. Holiness in the filth of sheep manure and sweat. Divinity entering the world on the floor of a stable, through the womb of a teenager, and in the presence of a carpenter.

She touches the face of the infant-God. *How long was your journey?*

The baby had overlooked the universe. These rags keeping him warm were the robes of eternity. His golden throne room had been abandoned in favor of a dirty sheep pen. And worshiping angels had been replaced with kind but bewildered shepherds.

God Came Near

Dear Lord, as amazing as it is that you would be born to Mary and be worshiped by shepherds, I am even more amazed that you would invite me to receive you into my life. I am overwhelmed by your grace and humbled by your humility. Gladly I offer my worship. In Jesus' name, amen.

14

MARY'S PRAYER

*But when the fullness of the time had come, God
sent forth His Son, born of a woman, born under
the law, to redeem those who were under the law,
that we might receive the adoption as sons.*

GALATIANS 4:4–5

God. O infant-God. Heaven's fairest child. Conceived by the union of divine grace with our disgrace. Sleep well. Sleep well. Bask in the coolness of this night bright with diamonds. Sleep well, for the heat of anger simmers nearby. Enjoy the silence of the crib, for the noise of confusion rumbles in your future.

Rest well, tiny hands. For though you belong to a king, you will touch no satin, own no gold. You will grasp no pen, guide no brush. No, your tiny hands are reserved for works more precious:

to touch a leper's open wound,

to wipe a widow's weary tear,

to claw the ground of Gethsemane.

Your hands, so tiny, so tender, so white—clutched tonight in an infant's fist. They aren't destined to hold a scepter or wave from a palace balcony. They are reserved instead for a Roman spike that will staple them to a Roman cross.

Sleep deeply, tiny eyes. Sleep while you can. For soon the blurriness will clear and you will see the mess we have made of your world.

You will see our nakedness, for we cannot hide.
You will see our selfishness, for we cannot give.
You will see our pain, for we cannot heal.
O eyes that will see hell's darkest pit and witness her
ugly prince . . . sleep, please sleep; sleep while you can.

God Came Near

Loving Father, your Son came into our broken
world to redeem us from our sin and make a way
for us to be adopted into your family. Thank you,
Jesus, for paying the price, for I was helpless to
pay it myself. Help me to live today as your child.
In Jesus' name, amen.

15

JOSEPH'S PRAYER

Then Simeon blessed them, and said to Mary His mother,
"Behold, this Child is destined for the fall and rising of
many in Israel, and for a sign which will be spoken against
(yes, a sword will pierce through your own soul also),
that the thoughts of many hearts may be revealed."

LUKE 2:34–35

God. O infant-God. Heaven's fairest child. Savor the sweet safety of my arms, for a day is soon coming when I cannot protect you.

Lie still, tiny mouth. Lie still, mouth from which eternity will speak.

Tiny tongue that will summon the dead,

that will define grace,

that will silence our foolishness.

Rosebud lips—upon which ride a starborn kiss of forgiveness to those who believe you, and of death to those who deny you—lie still.

And tiny feet cupped in the palm of my hand, rest. For many difficult steps lie ahead of you.

Do you taste the dust of the trails you will travel?

Do you feel the cold sea water upon which you will walk?

Do you wrench at the invasion of the nail you will bear?

Do you fear the steep descent down the spiral staircase into Satan's domain?

Rest, tiny feet. Rest today so that tomorrow you

might walk with power. Rest. For millions will follow in your steps.

And little heart . . . holy . . . pumping the blood of life through the universe: How many times will we break you?

You'll be torn by the thorns of our accusations.

You'll be ravaged by the cancer of our sin.

You'll be crushed under the weight of your own sorrow.

And you'll be pierced by the spear of our rejection.

Yet in that piercing, in that ultimate ripping of muscle and membrane, in that final rush of blood and water, you will find rest. Your hands will be freed, your eyes will see justice, your lips will smile, and your feet will carry you home.

And there you'll rest again—this time in the embrace of your Father.

God Came Near

O Lord, how can I ever thank you enough for giving your entire life that I might be kissed by forgiveness? You bore the thorns of my accusations and the piercing of my rejection. I rejoice that today I can follow in your steps. In Jesus' name, amen.

16

Too Busy to Notice the Impossible

He was in the world, and the world was made through
Him, and the world did not know Him. He came
to His own, and His own did not receive Him.

John 1:10–11

The noise and the bustle began earlier than usual in the village. Vendors were positioning themselves on the corners of the most heavily traveled avenues. Store owners were unlocking the doors to their shops. Children were awakened by the excited barking of the street dogs and the complaints of donkeys pulling carts.

The owner of the inn had awakened earlier than most in the town. After all, the inn was full, all the beds taken. Every available mat or blanket had been put to use. Soon all the customers would be stirring and there would be a lot of work to do.

One's imagination is kindled thinking about the conversation of the innkeeper and his family at the breakfast table. Did anyone mention the arrival of the young couple the night before? Did anyone ask about their welfare or comment on the pregnancy of the girl on the donkey? Perhaps someone raised the subject. But, at best, it was raised, not discussed. There was nothing *that* novel about them. They were, possibly, one of several families turned away that night.

Besides, who had time to talk about them when

there was so much excitement in the air? Augustus did the economy of Bethlehem a favor when he decreed that a census should be taken. Who could remember when such commerce had hit the village?

No, it is doubtful that anyone mentioned the couple's arrival or wondered about the condition of the girl. They were too busy. The day was upon them. The day's bread had to be made. The morning's chores had to be done. There was too much to do to imagine that the impossible had occurred.

God had entered the world as a baby.

Meanwhile the city hummed. The merchants were unaware that God had visited their planet. The inn-keeper would never believe that he had just sent God into the cold. And the people would scoff at anyone who told them the Messiah lay in the arms of a teenager on the outskirts of their village. They were all too busy to consider the possibility.

Those who missed his Majesty's arrival missed it not because of evil acts or malice; no, they missed it because they simply weren't looking.

Little has changed in the last two thousand years, has it?

God Came Near

Gracious Father, I am caught in the busyness of everyday life, and it is easy to miss what you are doing in my life today. Slow me down and open my eyes, Lord. Make your presence known that I may behold you doing the impossible. In Jesus' name, amen.

17

How Long
His Love
Lasts

For God so loved the world that He gave His
only begotten Son, that whoever believes in Him
should not perish but have everlasting life.

John 3:16

If you've ever wondered if anything separates us from the love Christ has for us, God answered that question before we asked it. So we'd see his answer, he lit the sky with a star. So we'd hear it, he filled the night with a choir; and so we'd believe it, he did what no man had ever dreamed. He became flesh and dwelt among us.

He placed his hand on the shoulder of humanity and said, "You're something special."

Untethered by time, God sees us all. From the backwoods of Virginia to the business district of London, from the Vikings to the astronauts, from the cave dwellers to the kings, from the hut builders to the finger pointers to the rock stackers, he sees us. Vagabonds and ragamuffins all, he saw us before we were born.

And he loves what he sees. Flooded by emotion. Overcome by pride, the Starmaker turns to us, one by one, and says, "You are my child. I love you dearly. I'm aware that someday you'll turn from me and walk away. But I want you to know, I've already provided a way back."

And to prove it, he did something extraordinary.

Stepping from the throne, he removed his robe of

light and wrapped himself in skin: pigmented, human skin. The light of the universe entered a dark, wet womb. He whom angels worship nestled himself in the placenta of a peasant, was birthed into the cold night, and then slept on cows' hay.

Mary didn't know whether to give him milk or give him praise, but she gave him both since he was, as near as she could figure, hungry and holy.

Joseph didn't know whether to call him Junior or Father. But in the end he called him Jesus, since that is what the angel had said and since he didn't have the faintest idea what to name a God he could cradle in his arms.

Don't you think their heads tilted and their minds wondered, *God, what are you doing in the world?*

"Can anything make me stop loving you?" God asks. "Watch me speak your language, sleep in your earth, and feel your hurts. Behold the Maker of sight and sound as he sneezes, coughs, and blows his nose. You wonder if I understand how you feel? Look into the dancing eyes of the kid in Nazareth; that's God walking to school. Ponder the toddler at Mary's table; that's God spilling his milk.

"You wonder how long my love will last? Find your

answer on a splintered cross, on a craggy hill. That's me you see up there, your Maker, your God, nail-stabbed and bleeding. Covered with spit and sin-soaked.

"That's your sin I'm feeling. That's your death I'm dying. That's your resurrection I'm living. That's how much I love you."

In the Grip of Grace

Gracious Lord, it's beyond my comprehension that nothing can separate me from your love . . . or that you love what you see when you see me. That you, my Maker and God, would die for me is a wonder. Thank you for opening the way back to you forever. In Jesus' name, amen.

18

SEEING JESUS

*So it was, when the angels had gone away from them
into heaven, that the shepherds said to one another,
"Let us now go to Bethlehem and see this thing that has
come to pass, which the Lord has made known to us."*

LUKE 2:15

God invites us to fix our eyes upon Jesus. Heaven invites you to set the lens of your heart on the Savior and make him the object of your life. But what does it mean to see Jesus?

The shepherds can tell us. For them it wasn't enough to see the angels. You'd think it would have been. Night sky shattered with light. Stillness erupting with song. Simple shepherds roused from their sleep and raised to their feet by a choir of angels: "Glory to God in the highest!" Never had these men seen such splendor.

But it wasn't enough to see the angels. The shepherds wanted to see the one who sent the angels. Since they wouldn't be satisfied until they saw him, you can trace the long line of Jesus-seekers to a person who said, "Let's go. . . . Let's *see*. . . ."

Not far behind the shepherds was a man named Simeon. Luke tells us Simeon was a good man who served in the temple during the time of Christ's birth. "And it had been revealed to him by the Holy Spirit that he would not see death before he had seen the Lord's Christ" (Luke 2:26). This prophecy was fulfilled only a few days after the shepherds saw Jesus. Somehow Simeon knew that the blanketed bundle he saw in Mary's arms was the Almighty God. And for Simeon, seeing Jesus was enough. Now he was ready to die. Some don't want to die until they've seen the world. Simeon's dream was not so timid. He didn't want to die until he had seen the Maker of the world. He had to see Jesus.

He prayed: "God, you can now release your servant; release me in peace as you promised. With *my own eyes* I've seen your salvation" (Luke 2:29–30 MSG, italics mine).

The Magi had the same desire. They wanted to see Jesus. Like the shepherds, they were not satisfied with the spectacular star they saw in the night sky. To be a witness of the blazing orb was a privilege, but for the Magi it wasn't enough to see the light over Bethlehem; they wanted to see the Light of Bethlehem. It was him they came to see.

And they succeeded! They all succeeded. More remarkable than their diligence was Jesus' willingness. Jesus wants to be seen! They were all welcomed. Search for one example of one person who desired to see the infant Jesus and was turned away. You won't find it.

I wonder if you would be willing to do the same. What matters is that you want to know Jesus. Since God "rewards those who truly want to find him" (Hebrews 11:6 NCV), he welcomes you to come today.

Just Like Jesus

O Lord, you are the Light of Bethlehem and the Light of my life. As I seek you, I want to see you and know you and fix my eyes upon you. I once was blinded by sin, but your grace has given me sight. May I behold you today in your beauty and glory. In Jesus' name, amen.

19

Too Majestic for Words

"She will bring forth a Son, and you shall call His name
Jesus, for He will save His people from their sins."

Matthew 1:21

Many of the names in the Bible that refer to our Lord are nothing less than palatial and august: Son of God, the Lamb of God, the Light of the World, the Resurrection and the Life, the Bright and Morning Star, Alpha and Omega.

They are phrases that stretch the boundaries of human language in an effort to capture the uncapturable, the grandeur of God. And try as they might to draw as near as they may, they always fall short. Hearing them is somewhat like hearing a Salvation Army Christmas band on the street corner playing Handel's *Messiah*. Good try, but it doesn't work. The message is too majestic for the medium.

And such it is with language. The phrase "There are no words to express . . ." is really the only one that can honestly be applied to God. No names do him justice.

But there is one name that recalls a quality of the Master that bewildered and compelled those who knew him. It reveals a side of him that, when recognized, is enough to make you fall on your face.

It is not too small, nor is it too grand. It is a name that fits like the shoe fit Cinderella's foot.

Jesus.

In the four gospels of the New Testament, it's his most common name—used almost six hundred times. And a common name it was. Jesus is the Greek form of Joshua, Jeshua, and Jehoshua—all familiar Old Testament names. When God chose the name his Son would carry, he chose a name so typical that it would appear two or three times on any given class roll. Were he here today, his name might be John or Bob or Jim.

He was touchable, approachable, reachable. And, what's more, he was ordinary. If he were here today, you probably wouldn't notice him as he walked through a shopping mall. He wouldn't turn heads by the clothes he wore or the jewelry he flashed.

"Just call me Jesus," you can almost hear him say.

He was the kind of fellow you'd invite to watch the football game at your house. He'd wrestle on the floor with your kids, doze on your couch, and cook steaks on your grill. He'd laugh at your jokes and tell a few of his own. And when you spoke, he'd listen to you as if he had all the time in eternity.

And one thing's for sure, you'd invite him back.

———

Those who walked with him remembered him not with a title or designation, but with a name—Jesus.

God Came Near

Dear Lord, the day is coming when at the name of Jesus every knee will bow and every tongue will confess that you are Lord. I bow my knee today and make my confession that you are my Lord. Help me to honor your great name above all else. In Jesus' name, amen.

20

What Love
Does

*. . . that Christ may dwell in your hearts through
faith; that you, being rooted and grounded in love,
may be able to comprehend with all the saints what
is the width and length and depth and height—to
know the love of Christ which passes knowledge; that
you may be filled with all the fullness of God.*

Ephesians 3:17–19

Would you do what Jesus did? He swapped a spotless castle for a grimy stable. He exchanged the worship of angels for the company of killers. He nursed from a breast and was clothed in a diaper.

If you were God, would you? I wouldn't, but Christ did.

If you knew that those you loved would laugh in your face, would you still care? If you knew that the tongues you made would mock you, the mouths you made would spit at you, the hands you made would crucify you, would you still make them? Jesus did.

He humbled himself. He went from commanding angels to sleeping in the straw. From holding stars to clutching Mary's finger.

Why? Because that is what love does. It puts the beloved before itself. Your soul was more important than his blood. Your eternal life was more important than his earthly life. Your place in heaven was more important to him than his place in heaven, so he gave up his so you could have yours.

He loves you that much, and because he loves you, you are of prime importance to him.

Love goes the distance . . . and Christ traveled from limitless eternity to be confined by time in order to become one of us. He didn't have to. Any step along the way he could have called it quits.

When he saw the size of the womb, he could have stopped.

When he saw how tiny his hand would be, how soft his voice would be, how hungry his tummy would be, he could have stopped. The first time he scraped his knee or tasted burnt bagels, he could have walked out.

When he saw the dirt floor of his Nazareth house. When Joseph gave him a chore to do. When his fellow students were dozing off during the reading of the Torah, his Torah.

At any point Jesus could have said, "That's enough! I'm going home." But he didn't.

He didn't, because he is love.

Think about that for a moment. Drink deeply from that for a moment. Don't just sip or nip. It's time to gulp. It's time to let his love cover all things in your life. All secrets. All hurts. All hours of evil, minutes of worry. His love will cover all of that. Every promise broken, drug taken, penny stolen. Every cross word, cuss word, and harsh word. His love covers all things.

Let it. Discover along with the psalmist: "He . . . loads me with love and mercy" (Psalm 103:4 NCV). Picture a giant dump truck full of love. There you are behind it. God lifts the bed until the love starts to slide. Slowly at first, then down, down, down, until you are hidden, buried, covered in his love.

Do it for his sake. For the peace of your heart.

And do it for their sake. For the people in your life. Let his love fall on you so yours can fall on them.

A Love Worth Giving

O Lord, you are divine love come down, and from you we have received grace and truth. Pour your love and mercy over me and cover all things in my life—my hurts and evil and secrets. I drink in your love for my every need. In Jesus' name, amen.

21

BE NUMBERED AMONG THE SEARCHERS

The Word became human and made his home among
us. He was full of unfailing love and faithfulness.
JOHN 1:14 NLT

The operative word of the verse is *among*. He lived *among* us. He donned the costliest of robes: a human body. He made a throne out of a manger and a royal court out of some cows. He took a common name—Jesus—and made it holy. He took common people and made them the same. He could have lived over us or away from us. But he didn't. He lived *among* us.

He became a friend of the sinner and brother of the poor. He touched their sores and felt their tears and paid for their mistakes. He entered a tomb and came out and pledged that we'd do the same. And to all of us frightened ones, he shared the same message: "Let not your heart be troubled; you believe in God, believe also in Me. . . . I will come again and receive you to Myself; that where I am, there you may be also" (John 14:1, 3).

And how do we respond?

Some pretend he doesn't exist. They occupy themselves with what they find in their part of the world and ask no questions about the Creator.

Others hear him, but don't believe him. It's not easy to believe that God would go so far to take us home.

But then, a few decide to give it a try. They venture

out of their corners and peek up through whatever opening they can find. Each day they look toward the sky. They, like Simeon, "wait for" and "look forward to" the day Christ comes (2 Peter 3:12 NCV). They know there is more to life than what they've found here, and they want to be ready when Christ comes.

Be numbered among the searchers, won't you? Live with an ear for the trumpet and an eye for the clouds. And when he calls your name, be ready.

Look up, and he will reach down and take you home . . . *when Christ comes.*

When Christ Comes

Father, I want to be among the searchers who are always seeking Jesus. That you have prepared an eternal home for me and want me to be with you is the best news I've ever heard. Ready my heart to find you. In Jesus' name, amen.

22

BLOODSTAINED ROYALTY

Mary kept all these things and pondered them in her heart.

LUKE 2:19

You mean to tell me God became a baby and was born in a sheep stable?" The one posing the question sounded as though he honestly didn't know if the story he was hearing was a legend or the gospel truth.

"That he would be raised in a blue-collar home, never write any books or hold any offices, be betrayed by his own people and executed like a common thief, buried in a borrowed grave, and be called the Son of God?" He paused a second. "Doesn't that all sound rather absurd?"

The Incarnation . . . absurd? Jesus on a cross . . . absurd? At the time, the man's questions had taken my Sunday school Jesus down from the flannel board.

Then it began to dawn on me: *What God did* makes sense. It makes sense that Jesus would be our sacrifice, because a sacrifice was needed to justify man's presence before God. It makes sense that God would use the Old Law to tutor Israel on their need for grace. It makes sense that Jesus would be our High Priest. *What God did* makes sense.

However, *why God did it* is absolutely absurd. When one leaves the method and examines the motive, the carefully stacked blocks of logic tumble. That type of love isn't logical; it can't be neatly outlined in a sermon or explained in a term paper.

Think about it. For thousands of years, using his wit and charm, man had tried to be friends with God. And for thousands of years he had let God down. He'd done the very thing he promised he'd never do. It was a fiasco. Even the holiest of the heroes sometimes forgot whose side they were on. Some of the scenarios in the Bible look more like the adventures of Sinbad the Sailor than stories for vacation Bible school. Remember the characters?

Aaron, the holy priest of God, leading the Israelites in fireside aerobics in front of the golden calf. David, the man after God's heart, getting his glasses steamed as a result of a bath on a roof. Adam adorned in fig leaves and stains of forbidden fruit. Moses throwing both a staff and a temper tantrum. King Saul looking into a crystal ball for the will of God. Noah, drunk and naked in his own tent.

These are the chosen ones to carry out God's mission? It's easy to see the absurdity.

Why didn't he give up? Why didn't he let the globe spin off its axis?

Even after generations of people had spit in his face, he still loved them. After a nation of chosen ones had stripped him naked and ripped his incarnated flesh, he still died for them. And even today, after billions have chosen to prostitute themselves before the pimps of power, fame, and wealth, he still waits for them.

It *is* inexplicable. And yet, it is that very irrationality that gives the gospel its greatest defense. For only God could love like that.

The question forced me to see Jesus as I'd never seen him. At first I didn't recognize him. But it was he. The lion. The Judean Lion. He walked out from among the dense trees of theology and ritual and lay down in a brief clearing. In his paw was a wound and in his mane were stains of blood. But there was a royalty about him that silenced even the breeze in the trees.

Bloodstained royalty. A God with tears. A Creator with a heart. God become earth's mockery to save his children.

How absurd to think that such nobility would go to such poverty to share such a treasure with thankless souls.

But he did.

In fact, the only thing more absurd than the gift is our stubborn unwillingness to receive it.

God Came Near

Lion of the tribe of Judah, I doubt that eternity will be long enough for me to ever figure out why you were willing to be stained with blood that I might live. But I thank you for your inexplicable love, and I receive it in silence and reverence. In Jesus' name, amen.

23

A Sacred Delight

*For you know the grace of our Lord Jesus Christ, that
though He was rich, yet for your sakes He became poor,
that you through His poverty might become rich.*

2 Corinthians 8:9

No man had more reason to be miserable than this one—yet no man was more joyful.

His first home was a palace. Servants were at his fingertips. The snap of his fingers changed the course of history. His name was known and loved. He had everything—wealth, power, respect. And then he had nothing.

Students of the event still ponder it. Historians stumble as they attempt to explain it. How could a king lose everything in one instant?

One moment he was royalty; the next he was in poverty.

His bed became, at best, a borrowed pallet—and usually the hard earth. He never owned even the most basic mode of transportation and was dependent upon hand-outs for his income. He was sometimes so hungry he would eat raw grain. He knew what it was like to be rained on, to be cold. He knew what it was like to have no home.

In his kingdom he had been revered; now he was ridiculed. His neighbors tried to lynch him. Some called him a lunatic. His family tried to confine him to their house.

Those who didn't ridicule him tried to use him. They

wanted favors. They wanted tricks. He was a novelty. They wanted to be seen with him—that is, until being with him was out of fashion. Then they wanted to kill him.

He was accused of a crime he had never committed. Witnesses were hired to lie. The jury was rigged. No lawyer was assigned to his defense. A judge swayed by politics handed down the death penalty.

They killed him.

He left as he came—penniless. He was buried in a borrowed grave, his funeral financed by compassionate friends. Though he once had everything, he died with nothing.

He should have been miserable and bitter. He had every right to be a pot of boiling anger. But he wasn't.

He was joyful. Joyful when he was poor. Joyful when he was abandoned and betrayed. Even joyful when he was hung on a tool of torture, his hands pierced with six-inch Roman spikes.

What type of joy is this?

I call it sacred delight.

It is sacred because it is not of the earth. What is sacred is God's. And this joy is God's.

———

It is delight because delight can satisfy and surprise.

Delight is Bethlehem shepherds dancing a jig outside a cave. Delight is Mary watching God sleep in a feed trough. Delight is white-haired Simeon praising God, who is about to be circumcised.

What is sacred delight? It is God doing what gods would be doing only in your wildest dreams—wearing diapers, riding donkeys, washing feet, dozing in storms. It's what you'd always dreamed but never expected. It's the too-good-to-be-true coming true.

Think about God's joy, which consequences cannot quench. There is a delicious gladness that comes from God that cannot be stolen. A sacred delight.

And it is within reach . . . in the person of Jesus.

The Applause of Heaven

Lord Jesus, you endured all that you did for the joy that was set before you; then you sat down at the right hand of your Father. I praise you that I can believe in you today and enter into an inexpressible and glorious joy. My delight is in you! In Jesus' name, amen.

24

COME AND
BEHOLD HIM

*What marvelous love the Father has extended to us! Just look
at it—we're called children of God! That's who we really are.*

1 JOHN 3:1 MSG

It's Christmas night. The midnight hour has chimed and I should be asleep, but I'm awake. I'm kept awake by one stunning thought. The world was different this week. It was temporarily transformed.

The magical dust of Christmas glittered on the cheeks of humanity ever so briefly, reminding us of what is worth having and what we were intended to be. We forgot our compulsion with winning, wooing, and warring. We put away our ladders and ledgers, we hung up our stopwatches and weapons. We stepped off our racetracks and roller coasters and looked outward toward the star of Bethlehem.

It's the season to be jolly because, more than at any other time, we think of him. More than in any other season, his name is on our lips.

And the result? For a few precious hours our heavenly yearnings intermesh and we become a chorus. A ragtag chorus of longshoremen, lawyers, illegal immigrants, housewives, and a thousand other peculiar persons who are banking that Bethlehem's mystery is, in reality, a reality. "Come and behold him," we sing, stirring even the sleepiest of shepherds and pointing them toward the Christ-child.

All of a sudden he's everywhere.

In the grin of the policeman as he drives the paddy wagon full of presents to the orphanage.

In the emotion of the father who is too thankful to finish the dinner table prayer.

He's in the tears of the mother as she welcomes home her son from overseas.

And he's in the solemn silence of the crowd of mall shoppers as the elementary school chorus sings "Away in a Manger."

Immanuel. He is with us. God came near.

It's Christmas night. In a few hours the cleanup will begin—lights will come down; trees will be thrown out. Size 36 will be exchanged for size 40; eggnog will go on sale for half price. Soon life will be normal again. December's generosity will become January's payments and the magic will begin to fade.

But for the moment, the magic is still in the air. Maybe that's why I'm still awake. I want to savor the spirit just a bit more. I want to pray that those who beheld him today will look for him next August. And I can't help but linger on one fanciful thought: If he can do so much with such timid prayers offered lamely in December, how much more could he do if we thought of him every day?

God Came Near

Gracious Father, I thank you that there are no limits to when you will come to us. You still come near, every day, when we come and behold you. Help me to focus the eyes of my heart on you today and take your presence with me wherever I go. In Jesus' name, amen.

25

A GLIMPSE OF HIS MAJESTY

For we did not follow cunningly devised fables when we
made known to you the power and coming of our Lord
Jesus Christ, but were eyewitnesses of His majesty.

2 PETER 1:16

It is amazing that we can live next to something for a lifetime, but unless we take time to focus on it, it doesn't become a part of our life. Think about it. One can live near a garden and fail to focus on the splendor of the flowers. A man can spend a lifetime with a woman and never pause to look into her soul.

And a person can be all that goodness calls him to be and still never see the Author of life.

Being honest and moral or even religious doesn't necessarily mean we will see him. No. We may see what others see in him. Or we may hear what some say he said. But until we see him for ourselves, until our own sight is given, we may think we see him, having in reality seen only a hazy form in the gray semidarkness.

Have you seen him?

Have you caught a glimpse of his Majesty? A word is placed in a receptive crevice of your heart that causes you, ever so briefly, to see his face. You hear a verse read in a tone you'd never heard, or explained in a way you'd never thought, and one more piece of the puzzle falls into place. Someone touches your painful spirit as only one sent from him could do . . . and there he is.

———

Jesus.

The man. The bronzed Galilean who spoke with such thunderous authority and loved with such childlike humility.

The God. The one who claimed to be older than time and greater than death.

Gone is the pomp of religion; dissipated is the fog of theology. Momentarily lifted is the opaque curtain of controversy and opinion. Erased are our own blinding errors and egotism. And there he stands.

Jesus.

Have you seen him?

Those who first did were never the same.

"My Lord and my God!" cried Thomas.

"I have seen the Lord!" exclaimed Mary Magdalene.

"We have seen his glory," declared John.

But Peter said it best. "We were eyewitnesses of his majesty."

His Majesty. The emperor of Judah. The soaring eagle of eternity. The noble admiral of the Kingdom. All the splendor of heaven revealed in a human body. For a period ever so brief, the doors of the throne room were open and God came near. His Majesty was seen. Heaven touched the earth and, as a result, earth can know heaven. In astounding tandem a human body housed divinity. Holiness and earthliness intertwined.

This is no run-of-the mill messiah. His story was extraordinary. He called himself divine, yet allowed a Roman soldier to drive a nail into his wrist. He sent men into all the world, yet equipped them with only bended knees and memories of a resurrected carpenter.

We can't regard him as simply a good teacher. His claims are too outrageous to limit him to the company of Socrates or Aristotle. Nor can we categorize him as one of many prophets sent to reveal eternal truths. His own claims eliminate that possibility.

Then who is he?

Let's find out. Let's follow his sandal prints. Let's sit on the cold, hard floor of the cave in which he was born. Let's smell the sawdust of the carpentry shop. Let's hear his sandals slap the hard trails of Galilee. Let's sigh as we touch the healed sores of the leper. Let's smile as we see his compassion with the woman at the well. Let's let our voices soar with the praises of the multitudes. Let's try to see him.

One warning. Something happens to a person who has witnessed his Majesty. He becomes addicted. One glimpse of the King and you are consumed by a desire to see more of him and say more about him. Pew-warming is no longer an option. Junk religion will no longer suffice. Sensation-seeking is needless. Once you have seen his face you will forever long to see it again.

My prayer for this book is that the Divine Surgeon has used it as a delicate surgical tool to restore sight. That blurriness will be focused and darkness dispersed. That the Christ will emerge from a wavy figure walking out of a desert image to become the touchable face of a best friend. That we will lay our faces at the pierced feet and join Thomas in proclaiming, "My Lord and my God." And, most supremely, that we will whisper the secret of the universe, "We were eyewitnesses of his majesty."

God Came Near

Heavenly Father, restore my spiritual sight to 20/20, that I might see your Son as he truly is and that I might know him for all that he is. May I proclaim him "my Lord and my God" just as truly as Thomas did. Help me to see more of him today. In Jesus' name, amen.

In The Manger
Sources Index

All of the material for *In the Manger* was originally published in books authored by Max Lucado. All copyrights to the original works are held by Max Lucado.

The Applause of Heaven (Nashville: Word, 1990): introduction, chapters 11, 23.

He Still Moves Stones (Nashville: Word, 1993): chapters 9, 10.

When God Whispers Your Name (Nashville: Word, 1994): chapter 5.

A Gentle Thunder (Nashville: Word, 1995): chapter 1.

In the Grip of Grace (Nashville: Word, 1996): chapter 17.

Just Like Jesus (Nashville: Word, 1998): chapter 18.

When Christ Comes (Nashville: Word, 1999): chapter 21.

A Love Worth Giving (Nashville: W Publishing Group, 2002): chapter 20.

God Came Near (Nashville: W Publishing Group, 2003): chapters 3, 4, 8, 12, 13, 14, 15, 16, 19, 22, 24, 25.

Next Door Savior (Nashville: W Publishing Group, 2003): chapters 2, 7.

3:16 (Nashville: Thomas Nelson, 2007): chapter 6.

About the Author

With more than 130 million products in print, Max Lucado is America's bestselling inspirational author. He serves the Oak Hills Church in San Antonio, Texas, where he lives with his wife, Denalyn, and their mischievous mutt, Andy.

The Lucado Reader's Guide

Discover . . . Inside every book by Max Lucado, you'll find words of encouragement and inspiration that will draw you into a deeper experience with Jesus and treasures for your walk with God. What will you discover?

3:16: The Numbers of Hope
. . . the 26 words that can change your life.
core scripture: John 3:16

And the Angels Were Silent
. . . what Jesus Christ's final days can teach you about what matters most.
core scripture: Matthew 20–27

The Applause of Heaven
. . . the secret to a truly satisfying life.
core scripture: The Beatitudes, Matthew 5:1–10

Before Amen
. . . the power of a simple prayer.
core scripture: Psalm 145:19

Come Thirsty
. . . how to rehydrate your heart and sink into the wellspring of God's love.
core scripture: John 7:37–38

Cure for the Common Life
. . . the unique things God designed you to do with your life.
core scripture: 1 Corinthians 12:7

Facing Your Giants
. . . when God is for you, no challenge is too great.
core scripture: 1 and 2 Samuel

Fearless
. . . how faith is the antidote to the fear in your life.
core scripture: John 14:1, 3

A Gentle Thunder
. . . the God who will do whatever it takes to lead his children back to him.
core scripture: Psalm 81:7

Glory Days
. . . how you fight from victory, not for it.
core scripture: Joshua 21:43–45

God Came Near
. . . a love so great that it left heaven to become part of your world.
core scripture: John 1:14

Grace
. . . the incredible gift that saves and sustains you.
core scripture: Hebrews 12:15

Great Day, Every Day
. . . how living in a purposeful way will help you trust more, stress less.
core scripture: Psalm 118:24

The Great House of God
. . . a blueprint for peace, joy, and love found in the Lord's Prayer.
core scripture: The Lord's Prayer, Matthew 6:9–13

He Chose the Nails
. . . a love so deep that it chose death on a cross—just to win your heart.
core scripture: 1 Peter 1:18–20

He Still Moves Stones
. . . the God who still does the impossible—in your life.
core scripture: Matthew 12:20

In the Eye of the Storm
. . . peace in the storms of your life.
core scripture: John 6

In the Grip of Grace
. . . the greatest gift of all—the grace of God.
core scripture: Romans

It's Not About Me
. . . why focusing on God will make sense of your life.
core scripture: 2 Corinthians 3:18

Just Like Jesus
. . . a life free from guilt, fear, and anxiety.
core scripture: Ephesians 4:23–24

A Love Worth Giving
. . . how living loved frees you to love others.
core scripture: 1 Corinthians 13

Next Door Savior
. . . a God who walked life's hardest trials—and still walks with you through yours.
core scripture: Matthew 16:13–16

No Wonder They Call Him the Savior
. . . hope in the unlikeliest place—upon the cross.
core scripture: Romans 5:15

Outlive Your Life
. . . that a great God created you to do great things.
core scripture: Acts 1

Six Hours One Friday
. . . forgiveness and healing in the middle of loss and failure.
core scripture: John 19–20

Traveling Light
. . . the power to release the burdens you were never meant to carry.
core scripture: Psalm 23

When God Whispers Your Name
. . . the path to hope in knowing that God knows you, never forgets you, and cares about the details of your life.
core scripture: John 10:3

When Christ Comes
. . . why the best is yet to come.
core scripture: 1 Corinthians 15:23

You'll Get Through This
. . . hope in the midst of your hard times and a God who uses the mess of life for good.
core scripture: Genesis 50:20

Recommended reading if you're struggling with . . .

FEAR AND WORRY

Before Amen
Come Thirsty
Fearless
For the Tough Times
Next Door Savior
Traveling Light

DISCOURAGEMENT

He Still Moves Stones
Next Door Savior

GRIEF/DEATH OF A LOVED ONE

Next Door Savior
Traveling Light
When Christ Comes
When God Whispers Your Name
You'll Get Through This

GUILT

In the Grip of Grace
Just Like Jesus

LONELINESS

God Came Near

SIN

Before Amen
Facing Your Giants
He Chose the Nails
Six Hours One Friday

WEARINESS

Before Amen
When God Whispers Your Name
You'll Get Through This

Recommended reading if you want to know more about . . .

THE CROSS

And the Angels Were Silent
He Chose the Nails
No Wonder They Call Him the Savior
Six Hours One Friday

GRACE

Before Amen
Grace
He Chose the Nails
In the Grip of Grace

HEAVEN

The Applause of Heaven
When Christ Comes

SHARING THE GOSPEL

God Came Near
Grace
No Wonder They Call Him the Savior

Recommended reading if you're looking for more . . .

COMFORT

For the Tough Times
He Chose the Nails
Next Door Savior
Traveling Light
You'll Get Through This

COMPASSION

Outlive Your Life

COURAGE

Facing Your Giants
Fearless

HOPE

3:16: The Numbers of Hope
Before Amen
Facing Your Giants
A Gentle Thunder
God Came Near
Grace

JOY

The Applause of Heaven
Cure for the Common Life
When God Whispers Your Name

LOVE

Come Thirsty
A Love Worth Giving
No Wonder They Call Him the Savior

PEACE

And the Angels Were Silent
Before Amen
The Great House of God
In the Eye of the Storm
Traveling Light
You'll Get Through This

SATISFACTION

And the Angels Were Silent
Come Thirsty
Cure for the Common Life
Great Day Every Day

TRUST

A Gentle Thunder
It's Not About Me
Next Door Savior

Max Lucado books make great gifts!
If you're coming up to a special occasion, consider one of these.

FOR ADULTS:

For the Tough Times
Grace for the Moment
Live Loved
The Lucado Life Lessons Study Bible
Mocha with Max
DaySpring Daybrighteners® and cards

FOR TEENS/GRADUATES:

Let the Journey Begin
You Can Be Everything God Wants You to Be
You Were Made to Make a Difference

FOR KIDS:

Just in Case You Ever Wonder
The Oak Inside the Acorn
You Are Special

FOR PASTORS AND TEACHERS:

God Thinks You're Wonderful
You Changed My Life

AT CHRISTMAS:

The Crippled Lamb
The Christmas Candle
God Came Near

Tools for your Church and Small Group

Because of Bethlehem/He Chose the Nails: A DVD Study

ISBN: 025986687847

$29.99

Max Lucado leads four video sessions that take small groups through *Because of Bethlehem* and the Advent season, a time of anticipation and celebration. And the story of Easter continues what Christmas began. In five additional sessions, Max unpacks the promises of the cross in *He Chose the Nails*, perfect for the Lenten season.

Because of Bethlehem
Study Guide

ISBN: 9780310687054

$9.99

In this four-session video-based study, bestselling author Max Lucado reveals that because of Bethlehem, we have the promise that God is always near us, always for us, and always in us.

Explore the Promises of Christmas in Color

ISBN: 9780718089788

$15.99

Bestselling author Max Lucado invites you to step out of the harried holidays and reconnect with the Christ of Christmas by meditating on the greatest gift ever given. As you add your personal touch to these inspirational Christmastime quotes, you'll discover joy and refreshment in the God who is always near you, always for you, and always in you.

"The King has come! Even for a little one like me."

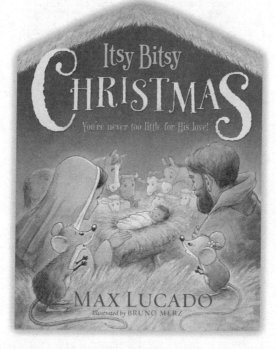

ISBN: 9780718088873

$8.99

For kids who feel too small or too ordinary comes a Christmas story that reminds us that Christ the King has come for everyone.

Experience Anew the Joy of Christmas

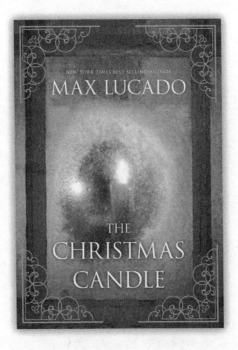

ISBN: 9781401689940

$16.99

Imagine a Victorian England village in the Cotswolds where very little out of the ordinary ever happens . . . except at Christmas time. This year, Edward Haddington, a lowly candle maker, is visited by a mysterious angel. That angel silently imparts a precious gift—a gift that's bungled and subsequently lost. When the candle maker and his wife finally find the gift, they face a difficult choice. Who among their community is most in need of a Christmas miracle?

Spread the Joy of Christmas

Celebrate the birth of Christ with a DaySpring® *Because of Bethlehem* Advent calendar, Christmas cards, and Christmas tree ornaments. Encourage someone special or treat yourself with these beautiful pieces you'll want to display at this time every year.

DaySpring.com

Christmas Music
from The Salvation Army

New York Staff Band
THE MESSAGE OF CHRISTMAS

1. Selection - The Message of Christmas (William Himes)
2. Intrada - Christmas Intrada (David Rowsell)
3. Christmas Day (Kevin Norbury)
4. Trombone Solo – Room in My Heart, soloist Brett Baker (Michael Kenyon)
5. Coventry Carol (William Broughton)
6. In Heavenly Peace (Terry Camsey)
7. March - Sounds Like Christmas (Norman Bearcroft)
8. The Wexford Carol (Dorothy Gates)
9. Adeste Fidelis (Franz Liszt, arr. Ronald Holz)
10. Christmas Angels (Kenneth Downie)
11. Cornet Solo - O Little Town, soloist Gordon Ward (Ralph Pearce)
12. The Festive Season (Paul Curnow)
13. Away in a Manger (William Broughton)
14. Celebrate the Season (Andrew Blyth)

Carolers' Favorites
133 CHRISTMAS CAROLS AND HOLIDAY SONGS

$ 9.95 Instrumental books
$ 19.95 Vocal/Score book

• Quality 4-part (optional 5th part) arrangements by Erik Leidzen, James Curnow & Stephen Bulla
• 18 Instrumental books available for Concert Band, Orchestra and Bass Ensemble – Part 1: Bb, Eb, C Part 2: Bb, Eb, C, F Part 3: Bb, Eb, C (Bass clef), F, Alto Clef Part 4: Bb, Eb, C (Bass clef) Part 5: Bb, C (Bass clef) Percussion
• Vocal and Instrumental books are compatible musically and numerically

Don't miss these stories from Max!

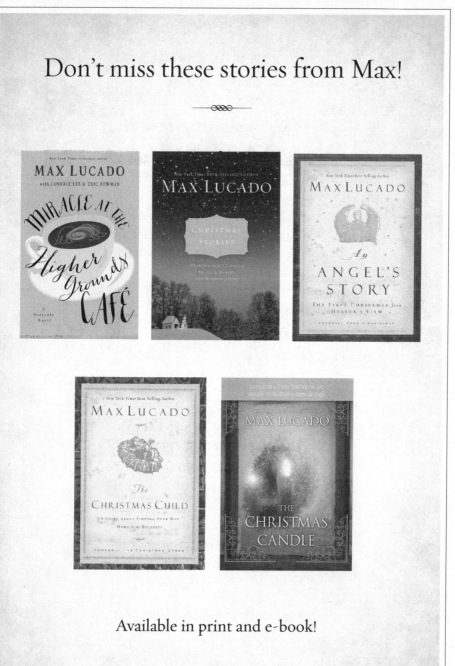

Available in print and e-book!

Inspired by what you just read?
Connect with Max.

Listen to Max's teaching ministry, UpWords, on the radio and online. Visit www.MaxLucado.com to get FREE resources for spiritual growth and encouragement, including:

- Archives of UpWords, Max's daily radio program, and a list of radio stations where it airs

- Devotionals and e-mails from Max

- First look at book excerpts

- Downloads of audio, video, and printed material

- Mobile content

You will also find an online store and special offers.

www.MaxLucado.com
1-800-822-9673

UpWords Ministries
P.O. Box 692170
San Antonio, TX 78269-2170